S - Amirsharafi -

30

Penguin Education

Success with English   The Penguin Course

General Editor

Geoffrey Broughton
Lecturer in English as a Foreign Language,
Institute of Education, University of London

Collaborating Committee

Alexander Baird
Lecturer in English as a Foreign Language,
Institute of Education, University of London

Geoffrey Barnard
Principal, St Katharine's College, Liverpool

J. A. Barnett
Director of Studies,
Regional Institute of English, Bangalore

Denis Cartwright
Principal Lecturer in English,
Cheshire College of Education, Alsager

Thomas Greenwood
Principal, Oxford Academy of English

Success with English   The Penguin Course

A First Reader

**Alexander Baird, Geoffrey Broughton,
Denis Cartwright and Gwyneth Roberts**

Illustrations by Maureen Roffey

Penguin Education

Penguin Education
A Division of Penguin Books Ltd,
Harmondsworth, Middlesex, England
Penguin Books Inc, 7110 Ambassador Road, Baltimore, Md 21207, USA
Penguin Books Australia Ltd, Ringwood, Victoria, Australia
Penguin Books Canada Ltd,
41 Steelcase Road West, Markham, Ontario, Canada

First published 1968
Reprinted 1970 (twice), 1971, 1972, 1974
Copyright © Alexander Baird, Geoffrey Broughton, Denis Cartwright and
Gwyneth Roberts, 1968

Designed by Arthur Lockwood

Made and printed in Great Britain by
Cox & Wyman Ltd, London, Fakenham and Reading
Set in Monotype Baskerville

Contents

John's busy telephone

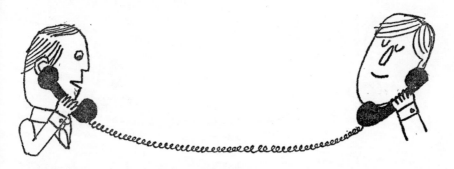

JOHN   Hello, this is John Clifton. Who's that?

DAVID   Hello, John. It's David. Listen. What are you doing on Saturday evening? Are you going out?

JOHN   No, I'm not going out on Saturday evening. I'm staying at home.

DAVID   Good. I'm going to a party at Helen's house. Are you sure you aren't going?

JOHN   No. I'm staying here and listening to my new records. But why?

DAVID   Well, John, I haven't got any shoes for the party. Have you got a pair of black shoes?

JOHN   Yes, I've only got one good pair of shoes, but they are black.

DAVID   Oh good. Please lend me them, John. We are old friends. You are staying at home on Saturday and I'm going to Helen's party. Please lend me your shoes.

JOHN   Oh, very well. Come and get them on Saturday afternoon. Good-bye.

DAVID   Good-bye, John.

JOHN   Hello, this is John Clifton. Who's that?

HARRY   Hello, John. This is Harry. Listen. Are you going out on Saturday evening? Are you going to Helen's or are you staying at home?

JOHN   No, I'm not going out. I'm staying here and listening to my new records. In my socks!

HARRY   Why are you listening to your new records in your socks?

JOHN   Oh, a friend hasn't got any black shoes, and I'm lending him my pair.

HARRY   Oh, you're a very good friend, John. Oh, John . . .

JOHN   Yes, Harry?

HARRY   Are you sure you're listening to your records on Saturday evening?

JOHN   Oh yes, I'm sure. Why?

HARRY   Well, I'm going to Helen's party and a lot of us are taking guitars. But I haven't got a guitar and you have. Please lend me your guitar for the party. You aren't practising on Saturday. You're listening to your records.

JOHN   Oh, very well. Come and get the guitar on Saturday afternoon. Good-bye.

HARRY   Oh, you're a very good friend, John. Good-bye.

JOHN   Hello, this is John Clifton. Who's that?

HELEN   Hello, John. This is Helen. Listen, I'm having a little party on Saturday evening and a lot of my friends are coming. I'm sure you've got a very good record-player.

JOHN   Yes, I have, Helen. But why?

HELEN   Well, my record-player isn't working. Please lend me yours.

JOHN   Very well, Helen. Are you coming here for it or – ?

HELEN   Oh, but you're coming to the party, John. Please come and bring your record-player with you. You're not going to the cinema or the theatre on Saturday, are you? Or practising the guitar?

JOHN   No, I'm not practising the guitar. Thank you.

HELEN   Oh, John, bring your record-player on Saturday afternoon.

JOHN   Oh, I'm sorry, Helen. David and Harry are coming here on Saturday afternoon.

HELEN   Well, bring it on Saturday evening. And bring your guitar with you, too. Good-bye, John.

JOHN   Good-bye.

JOHN   Now, what's Harry's telephone number? Perhaps he has got a pair of black shoes. And perhaps David has got a guitar.

The girl in the window

MAN   Hello. Is that Quickseats?

GIRL   Yes, it is. Good morning.

MAN   Good morning. I want to ask about planes from London Airport to Manchester.

GIRL   Oh, yes. One minute please. I'm getting the book. Yes, here it is. Do you want to fly in the morning or in the afternoon?

MAN   I'm not sure. When do the planes leave London?

GIRL   There's a plane in the morning. It leaves every day at ten o'clock. Then there's a plane at twenty minutes to two.

MAN   No, those are too early.

GIRL   Well, there's a plane at ten minutes to four.

MAN   Oh, yes, good. What time do these planes arrive in Manchester, please?

GIRL   The first plane leaves London at ten o'clock and arrives in Manchester at a quarter to eleven. The second plane leaves at twenty minutes to two and arrives at twenty-five minutes past two. And the third leaves at ten minutes to four and arrives at twenty-five to five.

MAN   Thank you. So, it takes forty-five minutes by plane.

GIRL   Yes, that's right.

MAN   Now, please, I want the times of trains from London to Manchester.

GIRL   Very well. Wait a minute, please. I'm getting the time-table. Yes, here it is. Now, what time do you want to go?

MAN   Is there a train late in the morning, or early in the afternoon?

GIRL   Yes, there's a train at lunch-time. It leaves London at twelve o'clock. And there's a second train at two o'clock.

MAN   Oh, good. And can I have lunch on the train?

GIRL   Yes, there's a restaurant car on the first train. People usually have lunch on that train.

MAN   Good. And what time do these trains arrive in Manchester, please?

GIRL   The twelve o'clock train arrives at twenty minutes to three and the two o'clock train arrives at twenty minutes to five.

MAN   Oh, thank you. So, it takes two hours and forty minutes by train and forty-five minutes by plane.

GIRL   Yes. Now do you want to fly or do you want to go by train?

MAN   Oh, wait a minute, please. How much are the tickets? Is the plane expensive?

GIRL   Just a minute. I'm getting the book again. Yes, here it is. By plane it's six pounds, four shillings from London to Manchester. And by train it's two pounds, ten shillings. Now, have you any more questions?

MAN   No, thank you.

GIRL   Good. Do you want to buy a plane ticket or a train ticket? – Hello, are you there? Are you listening?

MAN   Yes, I'm here. But I don't want a ticket. I'm not going to Manchester.

GIRL   Then why are you asking me a lot of silly questions?

MAN   Please don't be angry. I only want to talk to you. Every day I look through your window and you are there talking to people. You're very pretty and I want to talk to you again. Please, what time do you leave this evening?

GIRL   Oh, I usually leave here at half past five. But, I'm sorry. I have a husband and two children.

MAN   Oh, dear. I'm very, very sorry. Please excuse me.

GIRL   Listen. Are you there? I'm not the pretty young girl you look at every day through the window. That's Linda. Listen, stay there. Don't go away. Hello? Is that you, Linda? There's a young man here on the line. He wants to ask you about tickets from London to Manchester.

Three letters

35 Broad Street,
Newtown

16 March 1968

Dear Sirs,

On page twenty-two of your clothes catalogue there is a picture of your gloves. But the catalogue does not say what they are made of. Are they made of wool, or cotton?

I want a pair of gloves for working in. I work every evening in a bowling alley. Sometimes, when the machines are not working, I send the heavy balls back to the players. The gloves are for holding the balls and pins. Wool gloves are too warm for this. So please do not send me any gloves made of wool. I want a pair of strong cotton gloves size eight, not too heavy for wearing at the bowling alley.

I am sending you £1 (one pound) with this letter.

Yours faithfully,

Hilary Redhead

Top Drawer Clothes Ltd,
Highwood End,
Blackpool

18 March 1968

Dear Madam,

Thank you very much for your letter and the money. Thank you for telling us about our catalogue. We have gloves made of wool and gloves made of cotton, and we are putting a sentence about that in our new catalogue.

With this letter we are sending you a pair of our strong cotton gloves, size eight. Your letter does not say what colour you want, so we are sending a white pair.

Yours faithfully,

A.L. Jones

for
Top Drawer Clothes Ltd

Miss H. Redhead,
35 Broad Street,
Newtown

35 Broad Street,
Newtown

20 March 1968

Dear Sirs,

Thank you for your letter and the pair of gloves. They are very strong it is true but, I am sorry to say, they are too narrow for my hand. This is a pity, because the gloves are not too heavy or too warm for working in.

This pair is in a box which says, "White Cotton Gloves, Women's Size 8". But I am a man, so I want Men's Size 8. My name, Hilary, is a woman's name, but it is a man's name, too.

I am sending the gloves back to you. Please send me a man's pair.

Yours faithfully,

(Mr) Hilary Redhead

Eccles cakes

"Does Carolyn Carter live here? Is this Carolyn Carter's house, please?"

A photographer is standing near the front door of a big house and a young man asks him this question. The photographer isn't young, but his clothes are expensive. He's a good photographer and newspapers pay him a lot of money for his photographs.

But the young man is wearing cheap clothes. The day is cold and his hands are blue, because he hasn't any gloves. He's holding a cheap little case and a paper bag.

The photographer thinks this young man is a nuisance. "Carolyn Carter?" he asks. "Who's Carolyn Carter?"

"She's an actor," says the young man.

"Oh," says the photographer. "Is she a man? No? Then she's an actress, not an actor."

"I'm sorry," says the young man. "She's an actress, of course. Does she live here?"

"Wait," says the photographer. "Who do you think you are? She's Miss Carter, not Carolyn, to you."

The young man is tired and cold. He wants something to eat and he has too little money to buy anything. He says to the photographer, "Please tell her that Edgar is here."

"And who do you think I am?" asks the photographer. "Don't tell me what to do!"

"I'm sorry," says the young man. "I don't know who you are. Are you an actor? Please tell Miss Carter that Edgar's here."

The photographer is a clever man. He thinks that this young man is somebody special and that perhaps something is going to happen.

"Very well," he says. "This *is* Miss Carter's house and I'm going to tell her that you're here. Please wait for a minute or two. But tell me, who are you? Are you a friend?"

The young man doesn't answer the photographer's question. The photographer knocks at the door and the young man waits. He is cold and tired and hungry. The photographer knocks at the door again. This time an old man with grey hair opens the door. The photographer talks to him.

The old man looks at the photographer and then at the young man. "Come in," he says. "Miss Carter is at the theatre now, but she's coming back to the house at twelve o'clock. Please wait in the kitchen."

The old man takes the young man and the photographer into the kitchen and they sit there. The photographer is waiting too. He thinks that perhaps he's going to get a good photograph. There's a lot of food on the kitchen table. The actress is going to give a party. There are sandwiches and fruit on big and little plates. The young man is hungry and he looks at the food. But he doesn't want to think about food, and he looks away from it.

"So this is her house. It's very big," he says. The photographer looks at him but doesn't say anything.

The young man asks, "How many rooms are there in this house?" The photographer says that he doesn't know.

Edgar is thinking about Carolyn's old house in its narrow street. He thinks about the grey walls, the little windows and the cheap tables and chairs. He thinks about young Carolyn at seventeen, laughing because she has got a ticket for the theatre. Now people buy theatre tickets because they want to come and watch Carolyn, the actress. And today he is going to see Carolyn again – the new Carolyn. The photographer says something to him, but Edgar doesn't answer. He's thinking about old times.

"It's five minutes to twelve," the photographer says again. He gets up and walks about the kitchen. He opens the door.

The old man with grey hair comes to the kitchen door. "Please stay in the kitchen," he says, "and don't eat the food. Miss Carter's coming at twelve."

So the photographer sits down again. The young man is angry. Who is this old man with grey hair? Edgar thinks that when the old man knows about him and Carolyn he's going to be very sorry. Edgar opens his mouth to tell the old man that he is Carolyn's brother, but the old man goes away.

The young man looks at his hands. They are big, heavy hands, not an actor's hands, but they're good, strong hands. He hasn't got a very good job, but everyone in Eccles knows that he's Carolyn Carter's brother. Why doesn't Carolyn come to Eccles now? He's going to ask her that.

"Excuse me," says the photographer, "but what's in that paper bag?"

"This bag? Eccles cakes," says Edgar.

"What are Eccles cakes?" the photographer asks. Edgar doesn't answer. He thinks the photographer is stupid. He's hungry and he looks at the table again. Then he looks at the paper bag in his hands. But he's not going to eat Carolyn's party food and he's not going to eat the Eccles cakes. They're for Carolyn. Eccles cakes from home.

The photographer is listening to something. "Somebody's opening the front door," he says. "Miss Carter's arriving."

Edgar listens. There is a girl talking. Perhaps it's Carolyn, but he isn't very sure. He looks at his cheap clothes and he thinks for the first time that he isn't very smart. But now the old man is at the kitchen door.

"Miss Carter is home now," he says. "I'm going to tell her that you're down here in the kitchen and want to talk to her. Please tell me your name again."

"Edgar," says the young man.

"Edgar what?"

"Tell her Edgar's here. Edgar from Eccles," says the young man.

"Very well." The old man goes away again.

The young man and the photographer wait. The photographer is listening. The front door opens and shuts. The front door opens again and more and more people are talking, talking and laughing.

"It's going to be a big party," the photographer says. "Excuse me." He gets up and goes out of the kitchen.

The old man with grey hair comes into the kitchen. He doesn't look for the photographer. He has a lot to do.

"What does she say?" the young man asks.

The old man takes plates of sandwiches and fruit from the table, then he looks at the young man. "Don't sit there," he says. "Help me with these."

Edgar helps the old man. He takes some plates from the table. They go from the kitchen into a very big room. A lot of people are eating and drinking and laughing and talking. They take the food from the plates but they don't look at the old man or at the young man. The young man is looking for Carolyn, but she isn't there. Perhaps she's still in her room somewhere in the house. The plate in his hand is empty. He is going to stand near the wall and wait for Carolyn to come, but the old man comes up to him and says, "Go back into the kitchen and bring some more sandwiches."

The young man goes. When he's in the kitchen he hears people saying, "Carolyn! Carolyn! Hello, Carolyn!"

But now he doesn't want to go into the big room again. Somebody in there is laughing. It's Carolyn, he thinks. Why is she laughing? What is she laughing at? A lot of people are laughing. He thinks that someone says, "Eccles?" but he isn't sure. He sits on a kitchen chair and shuts his eyes.

The old man with grey hair comes into the kitchen. The photographer is with him now. They look at Edgar but they don't say anything.

Edgar looks up. "What does Miss Carter say?" he asks the old man.

The old man says, "This is a very big day for Miss Carter, you understand. She's giving a party. She says please wait here."

The photographer is asking himself if there's going to be a photograph or not. He doesn't want to wait for long. When the kitchen door is shut and the old man is in the next room, he says to the young man, "Tell me please. Who are you? What do you want with Miss Carter?"

"I'm Edgar," the young man says again. "I'm from Eccles. Eccles is Miss Carter's home."

The photographer is thinking that Miss Carter doesn't want to talk to this young man. Perhaps he's a friend of Miss Carter, but not a very good friend. Perhaps he has something to tell about her early days in Eccles and he's going to ask her for money. The photographer is a little sorry for Miss Carter, but he has his work to do as a newspaper man. So he sits down in the kitchen with the young man. They listen to the party in the next room. The photographer talks about Miss Carter.

"She's very beautiful," he says, "and a very clever actress."

"Is she?" the young man asks.

Sometimes the door opens and the old man comes from the next room to the kitchen and then goes back. Every time he comes in there are people talking and laughing near the door. The young man looks for Carolyn, but she isn't near the door. The old man doesn't say anything to him now, and Edgar thinks that now the old man understands who he is and is sorry for him.

The young man thinks, "She's never coming. London is her home, not Eccles. She's London's favourite actress now. I'm nobody. I'm not her brother now. She has no brother or mother or father now. We're a nuisance to her. We aren't as clever or as smart as she is. Our house is small and cheap. Her house is big and expensive. I don't think this house is comfortable, but perhaps Carolyn does. Her friends have got a lot of money. They give her expensive presents. I'm her brother and I bring her Eccles cakes. Why am I here?"

At first he is sorry for himself. Then he is angry with Carolyn. He stands up. The photographer looks at him.

"I'm going," says the young man. He puts the Eccles cakes in their paper bag on the kitchen table, and at that minute the kitchen door opens. But it's only the old man with grey hair.

The young man asks, "Is there a back door?"

"Yes," says the old man, "but aren't you waiting for Miss Carter?"

"No, I'm going now. Where's the back door? Show me."

The photographer is the only one in the kitchen now. He listens to the people at the party. Somebody is saying, "Excuse me for a minute, please." The kitchen door opens. It is Carolyn Carter. She's laughing at something. Her eyes are blue and warm. She is more beautiful than her photographs. She shuts the door and comes into the kitchen.

"Edgar?" she says. But there's no Edgar, only the photographer looking at her face.

"Where's my brother?" she asks.

Her brother! The photographer says, "He isn't here now. You're too late. Those cakes on the table are for you."

"Eccles cakes!" The actress takes them from the kitchen table. She opens the paper bag and takes out the cakes and puts them on an empty plate. She says nothing. She thinks that she is going to cry. Her blue eyes are full.

Now is the time for the photograph – that special photograph. The photographer holds his camera up. The actress looks at the camera. Now she understands why the photographer is waiting and looking at her. She doesn't cry.

"Eccles cakes. How silly!" she says. She laughs. And she goes back to the party.

The boy and his father

The boy and his parents live in New Street. The street runs down a long hill from Station Road. There are always lots of people in Station Road, but New Street is usually a quiet street and the people living there are quiet people. There are gardens with trees in them and on warm evenings the people of New Street talk to the people in the houses next to theirs. A lot of the people have children and on Saturdays and Sundays the children play in the gardens and in the street, so that Saturdays and Sundays are never quiet days.

The boy's name is David. He and his father are very good friends. On Sunday mornings, when his mother is in the kitchen and his father is looking at the newspaper, David reads. In the living-room there is a cupboard with glass doors and this cupboard is full of dirty old books. They are David's father's books, but his father doesn't read them now and his mother never reads anything. His brothers are older than David and they don't read the old books in the cupboard. They think David is stupid to read them, because the books are about mountains. They don't want to read about mountains.

So it is David who takes these books out of the cupboard on Sunday mornings and reads them or looks at the photographs of mountains in them. He doesn't understand what it is in these books that makes them his favourite books. There are other books in the house, but he doesn't read the others, only these. When he comes to the end of one of these books he shuts his eyes and thinks about mountains, and then the pictures come. In the pictures there is always one mountain. It is a special mountain. There are lots of mountain photographs in the books, but his special mountain isn't one of those. It is not a mountain, but the idea of a mountain, a mountain in his imagination.

Perhaps the idea of a mountain sometimes comes into his father's head too. They are his father's books. But the boy's father is a quiet man. He doesn't often talk about what he thinks. So the boy has the idea that he is the only one thinking about mountains, and perhaps this is true now.

Saturday afternoon is the time when the father takes the boy for a walk. They walk up and down the long streets past the little houses. On Saturday afternoons the boy understands his father and the father understands his son. They say very little but they are good friends. The father tells his son about his work. The boy tells his father about his teachers and his young friends. The man doesn't often laugh, but on Saturday afternoons, when he is with his son, then he sometimes does.

The boy doesn't want to think of this coming to an end. He understands that his father talks to him now because he is young. He understands too that one day his father is going to stop talking to him and laughing about his work and about the boy's teachers. His father doesn't often talk to his older sons and he doesn't go for walks with them. The boy thinks that perhaps his father talks to him now because the boy reads his books about mountains. Sometimes they talk about mountains and the father talks about the old days and his old friends, mountain climbers and walkers, and about mountains higher than any in England.

Where they live there are no mountains. But there are cold days when there is ice on the trees and it is very cold. On cold Saturday afternoons, as he walks with his father, the boy's nose and ears are red with the cold and he thinks about high mountains, white with ice and snow. He thinks that he's a climber in warm clothes and a fur hat and fur gloves. Sometimes the boy's mother and his brothers ask the boy and his father where they go on these cold Saturday afternoons. The boy and his father don't tell them, because they aren't sure. When they are walking through the streets they don't look at the houses and gardens. For David they aren't there. There is only the cold white mountain and he is always walking to it but never arrives at its foot.

One Saturday afternoon the boy and his father walk past a house with a very pretty garden. The boy stops and shows his father the garden. But his father only says, "Do you think that garden's pretty? The people in that house are as stupid as the people in the next house, and the garden's as ugly as the next garden!"

This is a new idea for the boy, that people are stupid. Because men and women are bigger and older than he is, he always thinks that they are cleverer too. But when his father talks, the boy always listens. This time it isn't easy to understand what his father is saying, but the boy wants to understand.

That night when he is in bed and his father and mother are saying good night to him, the boy asks his father, "People aren't always stupid, are they? I understand that there are bad people and silly people, but there are good people and clever people too. I think there are."

"Go to sleep," says his father. "Don't be silly."

But the boy doesn't go to sleep for a long time. He thinks that he doesn't understand his father, that he is too young to understand. Perhaps what his father says is true. But he understands that this is the end of those long afternoon walks with his father. He goes to sleep and in his sleep he is climbing mountains, high cold mountains.

Happy families

My grandparents are coming today, so I must get up early. My mother is making the breakfast and my father is walking up and down on the kitchen floor, saying "I am going to be late this evening. I've got a lot of work to do."

My mother is angry. "You're only saying that because my parents are coming."

"I've told you, I've got a lot of work to do."

"You've always got a lot of work to do when my parents come."

"That isn't true."

"Oh yes it is. You always say you must work late when my parents come; you are always late home then."

"I'm not going to talk to you when you're angry like this."

"Oh, I'm always wrong."

I come into the kitchen. "Is breakfast ready?"

"In a minute," says my mother. She puts the cups and plates on the table.

"Come home early from school today, and don't be late," she says. "Your grandmother and grandfather are coming."

"Yes," I say. "You have just told Father."

"Oh," says my mother; she is uncomfortable. "Well, eat your breakfast now, or you're going to be late for school."

When I come home in the afternoon, my grandparents are sitting in the living-room.

"Well, and how are you?" says my grandmother when she sees me. "Come here and say hello to your grandparents. How are you?"

My grandfather sees me, and says, "Ah, there you are. Have you had a good day at school?" He looks at me. "You're shorter than your cousin John," he says. "We can't have this. You must do something about it. Are you working well?"

"I always work well, Grandad," I tell him, looking at him with big eyes.

"Richard!" says my mother behind me. "Don't be silly. Go and wash your hands before tea. It's ready now."

My grandparents talk a lot at tea. First my grandmother talks, then my grandfather says that she has said something wrong, and then he talks for a long time. My mother says "Yes" and "No" sometimes, but I think she is waiting for my father to come home; she is very quiet.

When my father comes home (and he is early), he sees my grandparents' car in the road and walks into the garden at the side of our house, but my mother sees him and says, "Tom! Ah, I'm glad you're early, you're not too late to have tea with us."

"Good," says my father, but his face is very angry. He comes into the room and sits down at the table. Nobody speaks.

"Well," says my mother, looking at my father when we have finished tea, "I'm glad you're here now, you can talk to my father while we wash up."

She and my grandmother go out to the kitchen. My father and my grandfather sit in the living-room. Then my grandfather says, "Well, did you have a good day at work?"

They sit and talk for a few minutes, and then a second car stops outside the house. My father gets up, and goes to the door. He comes into the living-room, laughing. Behind him are my other grandparents – my father's parents. He goes to the kitchen, and tells my mother that they have come.

"Oh yes?" she says. "Good, I'm glad." She says this, but when I look at her face, I don't think she is very glad.

My other grandparents come into the room. My mother talks to her parents, my father talks to his parents, and the four grandparents talk to me.

Late in the evening my four grandparents leave the house. My parents say good-bye as they drive away. My mother says to my father, "Well, I'm glad they've gone."

He looks at her and says, "Are you talking about your parents or mine?"

She laughs. "Yours and mine." He laughs too. "I'm glad you're talking about yours as well as mine." They go into the house.

They are happy again, and I am too. But they are not glad that my four grandparents were here today – and I am very glad. My mother's parents have given me a pound, and my father's parents have too. There is a little aeroplane in a shop window near my school that I have wanted for a long time.

Every bad thing has some good in it . . .

Five bells

Robin was fifteen. He was usually a very active boy, but one Saturday morning, when his mother was washing up the breakfast things, he was sitting heavily in his father's comfortable chair, with his head in his hands. His father was reading the morning paper at the table and his older sister, Philippa, was in the hall, putting her coat on.

"What's wrong, Robin?" his mother said.

"Nothing," Robin said, "I've got a bad head."

"Oh dear, I'm sorry. Stay there in your father's chair," she said. But she was thinking, "That boy's working too late every night with his school work. I must buy him a little present this morning when I'm shopping."

Looking at Robin from his seat at the breakfast-table, his father was thinking, "He's done too much school work this week. He's a good boy. Perhaps I can find something for him when I'm at the shops this morning." And in the hall, Philippa was thinking, "Silly old Rob. What can I do for him? Sometimes, when I'm ill, he brings me a little present. Yes, that's a good idea. But what can I get him?"

Then Robin said, "I mustn't stay here. My bicycle bell's not working. I think it's broken, so I must mend it."

"Do that this afternoon," his mother said, "when your head's better." But she was thinking, "A new bicycle bell. I can get one at the cycle shop when I'm in the High Street." His father, going for his hat, was thinking, "That's a good idea. He wants a bell for his cycle. I can get one when I've been for my cigarettes." And Philippa, going out of the house was thinking, too. "Cycle bells are not too expensive. That's what I'm going to get him."

There were two doors in the bicycle shop, one in the High Street, and one in Bridge Street, because the shop was on the corner. At half past ten, Robin's father was in the shop, buying his son a new bell. "Thank you," he said to the assistant. "Five shillings? There. Thank you. Good morning." "Good morning, sir," the assistant said. But as Robin's father was going out of the Bridge Street door of the shop, Philippa was going in through the High Street door.

"Good morning," she said to the assistant. "I want a cycle bell, please. – Oh yes, that's a good one. How much is it? Five shillings?

Here you are," she said, giving him the money. "Good morning. Thank you."

"Thank you, Miss," the assistant said, but he was watching her leave through the High Street door, as her mother was coming into the shop through the other door.

"A bell, madam?" the assistant said. "Oh, yes. Here's a good one, look. We've sold a lot of these. They're very good and not very expensive. Noisy? Oh, no, they're not too noisy. That's what a bell is for, madam. They're only five shillings. Good. Thank you, madam. Good morning."

So, at a quarter to eleven, when Robin's mother was still shopping, with the new bell in her shopping-bag, Robin's father was arriving home again.

Robin was still sitting in the living-room, reading a book. "How's your head?" said his father, holding the new bell behind him. "Have you looked at your broken bell?"

"No," Robin said. "And my head's not too bad now, thanks."

"I'm just going into the garden for a minute," his father said. "There's something I must do."

At ten minutes to eleven the new bell was on Robin's bicycle, and the old one was in the dustbin. His father was coming back into the house from the garden as his mother was coming in with her shopping-bag. "I'm going out again," he said. "What's that in your hand?"

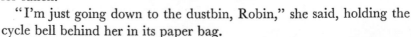

"Oh, nothing," Robin's mother said quickly. And as her husband went out she said, "Don't be late for lunch."

"I'm just going down to the dustbin, Robin," she said, holding the cycle bell behind her in its paper bag.

At eleven o'clock the second new bell was on Robin's bicycle and the first one was in the dustbin. His mother was coming in from the garden as Philippa was arriving home.

"Hello, Mother," she said. "Have you finished your shopping?"

"No, I haven't," her mother said. "I'm just going out again. But I'm coming back in twenty minutes. Good-bye."

Before she was in the street, Philippa was in the garden with her present. At ten minutes past eleven the third bell was on Robin's cycle and the second one was with the others in the dustbin.

Robin was still in the living-room. "I've just finished my book," he said to Philippa, "and my head's better now. Hey! Where are you going? Everybody's running in and out this morning. This house is like a bus station."

"I'm going back to help Mother," Philippa said. "Good-bye."

Watching her go down the street, Robin said, "Oh, well. It's a quarter past eleven and I still haven't looked at that broken bell. Come on, Robin, get on your feet."

"Well, the top of this bell isn't very dirty," he said, taking it off. "Perhaps it's dirty inside. No. Where's my knife? Perhaps I can push – Oh, now I've broken that little metal ring. Oh, dear. I mustn't tell the others I've broken it. They think I can mend it. Yes, I must go and buy a new bell. I can get to the shops on my cycle before they come back."

At half past eleven Robin was back home again with the fifth bell on his cycle. His mother, father and sister were arriving home too.

"Hello, Rob," his mother said. "Is your head better?"

"Yes, thanks," he said, laughing, "and my bell's working now. Listen." They were at the house door, watching him on his bicycle. His mother was thinking, "I'm glad his head's better. He likes his new bell." His father was thinking, "He likes his new bell. My present was a good idea. Now he's laughing." And Philippa was thinking, "Now he's laughing. He understands the bell's a present from me, but he doesn't want to talk about it. Boys are like that."

A bad day for Alfred

The manager opened the door of his office and went into the shop. The time was nine o'clock in the morning.

"Alfred," he said to a man in a white coat, "I've just telephoned the police station."

Alfred was the best assistant in the shop. He was a sensible, careful man.

"What did you tell them, Mr Jackson?" asked Alfred.

"I said that somebody, some thief, was taking things from our shop, and I said he was a very clever thief."

"What did they say at the police station, Mr Jackson?" asked Alfred.

"They said that this man was taking things from other shops too, not only our supermarket, and we must do what we can."

"That's true, Mr Jackson," said Alfred. "I'm going to watch people very carefully today."

"Good, Alfred, and please tell the other assistants. We must watch everybody in the shop. Perhaps the thief is coming again today."

And Mr Jackson, the manager of the supermarket, went back into his office.

Now it was past nine o'clock. The shop was open, and people were coming in with bags and baskets. It was Saturday, a day when a lot of people came to the shops to buy food for the week-end.

Most of these people were women, and some of them had little children with them. Children do not go to school on Saturdays, and their parents sometimes take them with them when they go to the shops.

Alfred was selling meat, and because he was working near the door he was carefully watching the people who were coming in.

"Mr Jackson has telephoned the police this morning," he said to the cashier. "He thinks that perhaps the thief is in here again today, because there are always a lot of people in the shops on Saturday."

"Do you think this thief is a man or a woman, Alfred?" asked the cashier.

"I think it's a man," answered Alfred. Then he went back to his work because three people were waiting for meat.

At ten o'clock everybody was working hard and the supermarket was full of people. Most of the assistants were running round with tins and boxes of food and drink and soap. When somebody took something from a shelf and put it in her basket, the assistant put a new tin or box on the shelf. Mr Jackson was walking round the shop. Everybody was working well, and the cashier was taking a lot of money. Mr Jackson was always happy when he saw a lot of money in the drawer in the cashier's table.

At eleven o'clock, Alfred, his hands full of meat, saw a man near the shop door. He was wearing dark clothes, dark glasses, a soft hat over his eyes, and he had a big basket in his hands. Alfred saw that the man had very big pockets. He was taking things from the shelves and putting them back again. When people came near to him he looked away from them. Now he was walking slowly to the other end of the supermarket.

Alfred saw Mr Jackson standing behind some women who were buying fruit.

"Excuse me, please, for a minute," Alfred said to a woman who asked for some meat. He went up to Mr Jackson.

"Do you see that man over there, in the soft hat?" he said. "I think there is something wrong with him, Mr Jackson."

"Where?" said the manager.

"There, in the dark glasses, near the butter."

"Now I see him, Alfred," said the manager. "Thank you. Perhaps this is the man we want."

Mr Jackson watched the man carefully for five minutes. Then he went back to Alfred.

"I'm sure he's a thief," he said. "Alfred, I'm going to telephone the police. You wait here. He mustn't leave the shop." And he went into his office.

Three minutes later Alfred saw the man coming to the door. Mr Jackson was still in his office. The man was leaving the shop! Alfred went up to him.

"You can't leave this shop," he said to the big man in dark glasses, who was standing in front of him. "Stop!"

But the man did not stop. He put his hand on the door of the shop.

"Stop!" said Alfred again. Then he quickly took a big piece of wet red meat, and hit the man in the face with it!

Then two doors opened, the door of the shop and the door of the manager's office. At one door was a policeman in a big helmet, and at the other door was Mr Jackson.

"That's the man!" said Alfred to the policeman. He was still holding the piece of meat.

They looked down at the man on the floor. His glasses were broken, and there was blood on his face – blood from the meat and from his nose.

The policeman put a big hand on the man's shoulder.

"You come with me, my man," he said.

Everybody was standing round, men, women, children, and the assistants too. The man was on his feet now, with his hand to his nose.

"Don't be silly, William," he said to the policeman. "It's me."

The policeman looked carefully into his face. Nobody said anything for a minute.

The policeman in the helmet then said to Mr Jackson, "You've got the wrong man here. This man is from the police station, like me. He was watching for the thief in your shop, Mr Jackson. He was on a special job."

"Oh," said Mr Jackson.

"Now," said the policeman in the helmet. "Where is the man who hit this policeman in the face with a piece of meat?"

"Here I am," said Alfred, "I'm very sorry I hit him."

"Don't do it again!" said the policeman. "We're going back to the police station now, Mr Jackson. Please telephone us again when you're sure you have found the thief. Come on, William." And the two men went out of the door.

"Back to work, back to work, everybody!" said Mr Jackson, and then went into his office.

One minute later Alfred put his head round the door.

"Come quickly, Mr Jackson!" he said.

"What's wrong, Alfred?"

"When the policeman was here," said Alfred, "somebody took the best pieces of meat, and all the notes from the drawer in the cashier's table, ninety-five pounds!"

Three more letters

X

16 Greenford Avenue,
Kingston

Saturday

My darling Caroline,

I can't stop thinking about you. Last night, when we danced and you were in my arms for the first time, it was the happiest day of my life. When I think of the other girls I have danced with, I know that you are the most beautiful girl I have ever known. I never want to dance with any other girl; I never want to walk home with anybody else. Last night when I was with you it was – oh, I don't know how to write it. I don't know what to say. You see? When I'm not with you I'm lost for words. I only want to be with you and talk to you, but you say you can't see me again before next Saturday. That's seven days, a hundred and sixty-eight hours! I've looked at the clock a hundred times today, but the time goes so slowly.

I can't wait for next Saturday. When you get this letter on Monday, please write back. If I can't see you and talk to you, a letter is the next best thing. I haven't started the book you lent me, but it's at the side of my bed and I'm going to read it tonight. Every word from beginning to end, because it's yours.

I love you, I love you. There, I've said it. Please, please write back.

With all my love,
Yours,

best wishes
see you soon. Charles

P. S. There's a very good film on at our cinema next week.

all the best

P.S = e C T

35

16 Greenford Avenue,
Kingston

Tuesday

Dear Caroline,

I wrote to you on Saturday – did you get the letter? I asked you to write back, but there was no answer from you this morning. Perhaps you don't like writing, or perhaps you are ill. I wasn't going to write again: I was going to wait for your letter. But then I suddenly thought – perhaps she's ill. Please write a few words to tell me you're well.

And there's another thing. I've started reading your book – I haven't finished it yet, but it's very good. The thing that's worrying me is the writing inside the front cover. It says "To my dearest Caroline. Love from Ken." I know I'm silly. But please, who is Ken? Perhaps he's your brother, or I've told myself that perhaps he's an old friend. The trouble is the book's very new. Or perhaps it's not your book – perhaps Caroline is your mother's name and the book's hers.

When I wrote to you on Saturday I said I couldn't stop thinking about you. But now I've started reading your book and I can't stop thinking about you and this Ken. I know there's an easy answer to this and I know I'm going to see you on Saturday. But I can't wait for then. Please write a few words. I'm so unhappy.

Love,

Charles

P. S. Do you want to go to the cinema?

16 Greenford Avenue,
Kingston

Friday

Dear Miss Perkins,

Thank you for your letter. I can see now that I've been very silly and I know that I was wrong in what I thought about you. But I am not going to write another letter for you to laugh at. I only want to say that I fully understand that you are not coming out with me tomorrow night.

I'm sending your book back with this letter. I haven't finished reading it – but it's not very good. As you know, I've written two other letters to you – please may I have them back?

Yours sincerely,

Charles Ford

Emergency at the airport

"Hullo, John, you're early this morning," said Bill.

"Yes, I am," said John. "Usually I come in the train from home and then in the bus to the airport, but today I came in my car."

"Did you leave it in the airport car park?"

"Yes," said John, "in front of the restaurant. I had a cup of tea there before I came up."

The two men, Bill and John, worked at London Airport. They sat in front of the radar machines in a high room in the airport buildings and looked down through the big windows at the planes, the cars, the buses and the people.

"It's very warm in here," said John. "Outside it is cold, and there is ice on the ground." They looked at the men who worked round the aeroplanes. They had warm clothes. Some of them wore their hats down past their ears, and they all had big gloves on their hands. They worked under a heavy grey sky. Passengers came down from the big hall of the airport and got into a bus which took them to their plane. They walked from the bus to the metal stairs which led up to the doors of the plane. Airport men put the cases of the passengers through a hole in the side of the plane. When the cases were in they closed the door over the hole, took the stairs away and shut the passenger doors too. The buses and cars drove away, as well as the men.

Now Bill and John were working in their room. They told the pilot of the plane that it was time to go. Very slowly, the heavy plane started from the airport buildings, up to the end of the airport.

"There are no planes in the sky near the airport now," said Bill.

"You can go," said John to the pilot.

The plane went very slowly, then faster and faster down the runway, in front of the airport buildings. Friends of the passengers lifted their hands, waving.

"Good-bye, good-bye," they shouted.

The plane was going very fast now. The pilot pulled the nose of the plane up and the plane slowly left the ground and climbed into the heavy grey sky. For a moment Bill and John saw its white and red wings, then suddenly it was gone.

John was still talking to the pilot. There was no fault in the plane.

The equipment was working, but the pilot could not see in front of the plane, and there was ice on the wings.

"The ice is very bad up there this morning," John said to Bill. "That Istanbul plane's climbing through cold rain, and there's heavy ice on the wings."

"Is he in trouble? Is his equipment working?" asked Bill.

The pilot was speaking again. The plane was safe now. The equipment was throwing the ice off the wings and the plane was climbing easily.

Bill and John worked quietly through the day. At eleven o'clock they drank cups of coffee and ate sandwiches. Planes came and went. Upstairs in their warm room they talked quietly to the pilots in their planes, and watched the radar, which showed them where the planes were in the sky.

At one o'clock they went down to the restaurant for their lunch.

"It's raining harder now," said Bill as he looked out of the window.

"Good," said John. "It's going to be warmer this afternoon."

"Perhaps," said Bill. "It's raining, but there's still ice on the ground, and that's dangerous."

"That's true," said John. "Drink your coffee. We must get back now."

"I'm ready."

They went back to their work. The time was now two o'clock. The clouds were heavier and the rain was still falling. On the airport the ground was cold and the ice did not go.

John was talking to the pilot of an American plane flying from America to London.

"Is that plane PA 634 coming?" asked Bill.

"Yes, I'm talking to him now. He's going to arrive in thirty minutes, and he's an hour late."

Bill spoke over the telephone to the girl down in the airport passenger hall, "PA 634 is one hour late."

The girl spoke to the people who were waiting for the plane, "PA 634 from America is one hour late. Please sit down and wait in the airport hall. The plane is going to arrive at four o'clock. Thank you."

Suddenly Bill said, "I have got him on the radar now."

"We can see you on radar now, PA 634," said John to the pilot.

"Thank you, London," said the pilot. "It looks black and dirty down there. Is the airport open?"

"Yes, the airport's open. It's raining here and cold. There's ice on the ground."

"Hello, London," said the pilot. "This is going to be difficult. Can you still see me on radar?"

"Yes, we can see you. You're in line now."

"I'm coming down. I'm starting now," said the pilot. Then he said, "It's black in front of me and raining hard."

"We can see you on radar," said John. "You are coming down easily."

Bill suddenly shouted, "He is going too low. Tell him! He is too low!"

"Hello, PA 634, you are too low. Climb higher, quickly."

"Hello, London, There's heavy ice on the wings."

"Your speed is too slow, PA 634. Go quicker and climb."

Quietly Bill and John watched the radar.

"Is he right now?" asked John.

"He's climbing very slowly," said Bill.

"Look through the window!" said John. "The sky's black and it's raining harder. This is very dangerous. There's ice on the wings and ice on the ground. And he can't see the ground!"

"He must climb and go away. The airport isn't safe for him. Tell him quickly!" said Bill.

"Hello, PA 634," shouted John. "You cannot come in. Climb away! Climb away!"

"Hello, London," said the pilot quietly, "I can't climb. I'm too low and the ice is heavy. There's a fault in the de-icing equipment. It isn't throwing the ice off. I must come in!"

Bill was speaking through the telephone to the Airport Fire Station, "Emergency! Emergency! PA 634 is coming in. There's heavy ice on the wings. He's going to hit the ground hard!" Then he pushed the red button on his table. Emergency bells rang in the airport buildings.

"Hello, PA 634," said John. "We're ready for you now. We can see you on the radar. You're still low. Climb! Go higher! That's right. Come in like that. You're dropping again! Go higher. That's right. Come in like that."

"Fire Station! PA 634 is one minute from the airport," said Bill through the telephone. Then he looked through the windows at the airport. "I can see him! I can see him!" he shouted.

The big plane was dropping out of the grey sky.

"Can you see the ground?" John said to the pilot. "We can see you now."

"Yes, I see the ground. I am putting the plane down . . . NOW!"

Bill looked out of the window at the plane. "He's coming in fast, too fast," he said.

"He has put the plane down. He's stopping," said John.

"But there's ice on the ground."

"He has stopped down at the end of the airport where the firemen are. He's safe. He's coming back now to the terminal building," said John.

Bill sat down in his chair and shut his eyes.

"Are you ill?" asked John.

In the air terminal building the girl was speaking to the people. "Plane PA 634 from America has arrived. Friends of passengers please wait in the hall of this building. Thank you."

"PA 634 to London Airport," said the pilot to John. "We hit the ground fast, but we are safe. Thank you."

Bill and John went down from the radar room. They finished their work for the day.

"I am going to take you home," said John. "Get in the car."

Bill's face was still white. "Be careful," he said. "There is ice on the road." John laughed and drove slowly back to London to Bill's house. It was still raining.

Under the high trees

At six o'clock on Wednesday evening Ben Smith arrived home from the school where he was a teacher. His wife, June, met him at the door of the house.

"Ah, here you are, Ben. I'm glad you're home. You're just in time."

Ben Smith shut the door of his old car. "In time for what?" he asked.

"Ben, have you forgotten? We're going out. We're going to the theatre. Penny is ready." Penny was their sixteen-year-old daughter. Ben was tired and he did not understand.

"Is Penny going to the theatre too?" he asked.

"Oh, you are silly," said his wife. "She's staying at home with Rodney." Rodney was their small son. "She's just giving him his supper. She's going to put him to bed when we leave. Now go and put your other clothes on. Your supper's ready. Please be quick, Ben."

Later, when Ben was eating his supper, he said, "Must we go out, June? I'm very tired. There was a lot of work and trouble at school today."

June looked at him and said nothing. Inside, she was very angry. Finally she said, "You're always tired. We never go out. Every night you read or watch the television. Or you sit in your chair and say nothing. Well, tonight we are going out. We've got seats at the theatre. I've got the tickets. Now eat your supper."

Ben quietly ate his supper. What his wife said was true. They did not often go out in the evenings. Suddenly he was sorry for her, so he quickly finished his supper.

"Leave the plates and cups," said his wife, "Penny's going to wash up." She looked into the bedroom. "We're going now, Penny. Is Rodney happy?"

"Yes, Mother," said Penny from the bedroom. "He has drunk his milk and now I'm going to read him a story."

"Good-bye, Penny," said her father.

Ben Smith and his wife stood by the old car in front of their house. They got in. Ben switched on and pushed the starter button. Nothing happened. He pushed again. Again there was nothing. June pushed the button too.

"Oh, Ben!" she said.

"It's no good. There's no petrol," said Ben. "Now we can't go to the theatre."

"Yes, we can. We can go on the bus. Come on!"

They got out of their car and ran up the road. At the end there was a bigger road, and a lot of cars and buses were going up and down.

"It's better by bus," said June. "There's no car park near the theatre."

"What time is it now?" asked Ben.

"It's fourteen minutes past seven," said June, "and we want a number 64 bus."

"We're going to be late," said Ben sadly. Buses came down the road, and stopped, but they were not the right buses for Mr and Mrs Smith. A number 27 bus stopped. People got on and people got off. The bus drove away. Then came a number 42. Ben's nose and feet were cold. He put his hands in his pockets and said nothing. Finally a number 64 bus stopped at the bus-stop.

The seats were full. Ben and June stood with six other people inside the bus. The bus conductor came with the tickets. "You must get off, Mister," he said to Ben. "Only seven people can stand in this bus. That's the law."

"But I'm with my wife," said Ben, "and we're going to the theatre."

"You can go to New York with her," said the man, "but not on my bus." And he rang the bell. The bus stopped suddenly.

"You stay on the bus," shouted Ben to his wife as he got off.

"But I've got the theatre tickets!" she shouted back. Before Ben could answer the bus drove away. He forgot about the tickets because it was raining. The road was wet and there was a hole in his shoe. A number 64 bus stopped and he got on. This time there was a seat. He paid a shilling for his ticket and then shut his eyes. When he opened them again the bus was past the theatre. He rang the bell and the bus stopped suddenly. It was still raining as he walked back to the theatre and went in through the big doors. He saw photographs of the actors, and over the doors were the words "UNDER THE HIGH TREES".

"Tickets, please," said the man at the door. Ben put his hand in his pocket but there was nothing there. June had got his ticket in her bag, and she was inside the theatre.

"My wife has got my ticket," explained Ben.

"I don't understand," said the man at the door.

"She's in the theatre. She's got my ticket."

"Which seat is she sitting in? Is it upstairs?" asked the man.

"I'm sorry, I don't know," said Ben uncomfortably, and he did not know what he could do. He stood by the door for a moment. As he was going out into the street a girl behind the ticket-office window said, "Are you Mr Smith? I've got your ticket. Your wife left it with me."

"Oh, thank you!" said Ben, and the man at the door showed Ben to his seat. It was in the middle of the theatre. He pushed past people who were sitting down.

"Excuse me. Excuse me, please," he said. He heard the words of people round him.

"Oh dear!"

"Please don't be so noisy!"

"Sit down!"

"It's not right to come into the theatre after the play has started."

Ben's face was red. He stood on a man's foot. "Sorry," he said. Then he found his seat.

"You're late," said his wife.

"Quiet!" said the people to the left and to the right of them.

Ben and his wife sat and watched. Ben's shoes were still wet. He listened to the actors but he could not understand the story. One actor, an old man, spoke very quietly, and the other, a young man, spoke very quickly.

After about half an hour Ben asked his wife, "Can you understand the story?"

"No, Ben," she said, "and I can't see very well. There is a big man in front of me."

"It's awful," said Ben, "and I haven't been warm since I left home. My feet are wet too."

For a long time they sat in their seats. Ben closed his eyes again, but he was hungry as well as cold. He thought of plates of new bread and cheese and glasses of strong beer, and this made him happier.

Suddenly it was finished. People round them stood up. "Come on!" said Ben. "Run for the number 64 bus!"

They ran out of the doors of the theatre to the side of the road. There were no buses, and it was raining. They waited and waited for the bus, and their clothes got wetter. Finally Ben shouted, "Taxi!"

A taxi stopped. Ben pushed his wife in.

"50 Wood Road, past the Police Station," said Ben to the taxi driver.

"Thank you, Ben," said June, as she sat in her wet clothes and watched the houses and shops through the windows of the taxi.

The taxi went slowly up Wood Road, "Here?" asked the taxi driver.

"Yes," said Ben. The taxi driver did not get out, so Ben opened the door for his wife.

"Give me the key of the house. You pay the driver," she said.

The driver pushed down his window. "Two pounds," he said.

"What?"

"After ten o'clock in the evening, two pounds," said the taxi driver. Ben took the money slowly out of his pocket.

"You're a thief," he said sadly. He watched the taxi as it drove down the street, and quietly said a few strong words to himself. This made him happier inside.

Penny was in the kitchen when Ben came into the house.

"Two pounds for the taxi," he said. "The end of a happy evening."
His wife said nothing. She was making coffee.

"Did you watch television?" Ben asked his daughter.

"Yes," she said. "The play has just finished, and it was very good."

"Did you hear the words? Did you understand what the actors said?"

"Oh, yes."

"And did you understand the story?" he asked.

"Yes, it was easy," she said.

"What was the name of it?" asked Ben as he picked up his cup of coffee.

"'Under the High Trees'," she said.

Ben Smith put his cup of coffee on the kitchen table and went slowly upstairs to bed.

Always carry a camera

On Saturday mornings the big public library opens at half past nine. A lot of people go into the library on Saturday because this is the time when they go shopping for their food. When they have done their shopping, they take their books into the library, and go home with new ones.

Susan and Margaret, the two girl assistants, were standing behind the library desk. They took books from the people who came in, and gave them their tickets. It was a warm Saturday, and a lot of people were in the streets and in the shops, and many were coming into the library too.

"Where's Ann this morning?" asked Susan. She was taking books from the desk and putting them on the trolley.

"She's been ill," said Margaret. "I don't know what's wrong with her, but the doctor's going to see her today."

"Who told you?" asked Susan.

"The Head Librarian. Ann's mother telephoned him yesterday. He told me just before you arrived this morning."

"Well," said Susan, "he knows that there are always a lot of people on Saturdays. Usually we have three assistants, but now Ann's ill and two of us can't do the work." Already a line of people were standing at the desk. They were waiting for their tickets.

"When there's a lot of work, he always sits in his office." Susan did not like little Mr Day, the Head Librarian. The assistants laughed at him when he was out of the room.

Susan saw that the trolley was full of books, and she pushed it down the library and put the books back on the right shelves. She worked hard, and in ten minutes the trolley was empty. Then she saw that more and more people were waiting at the desk. Some of them were waiting to go out with their new books. Susan worked quickly. In the book was a little pocket, and in this pocket a piece of paper, with the name and number of the book on it. Susan took this piece of paper out of the pocket in the book. She put the date on the piece of paper and on the right page of the book. Then she put the piece of paper in the person's ticket, which was like a little envelope. Then, at the end of the day, the assistants put the tickets in the right order in the drawers of their desks.

When Susan went back to Margaret, she saw a young policewoman at the door.

"Excuse me, please," said the young policewoman. She pushed through the people and came up to the desk.

"It's Mary," said Margaret. "Hello, Mary." The two assistants knew Mary. They were the same age, and sometimes they went out with her in the evenings. "What book do you want?"

"I don't want a book," said the young policewoman. "I've come about the man who took the money from that train near London in January. I must see Mr Day."

Susan laughed. "Is Mr Day the thief?" she asked. "He's in his office. He always *is* in his office when we have a lot of work to do in the library. Come round this side of the desk." The two girls went to the door of Mr Day's office. Susan knocked.

"Come in," said the man inside. Susan opened the door. Mr Day sat behind a mountain of new books. He was writing a list of them.

"Mr Day," said Susan, "there is a policewoman here. She has come about a thief."

"Send her in and give this list of new books to Margaret," said Mr Day. Mary went into Mr Day's office, and Susan went back to the people at the desk.

"I knew he was that thief," said Susan. "He bought a new car in February, and a lot of new clothes."

"Don't be silly," said Margaret. "It wasn't in February, it was in April, the month we got more money."

"That horrible green shirt with the blue and yellow tie," said Susan. Margaret laughed.

"Hello," said a young man. He stood at the desk with twelve books under his arm. He was wearing a white shirt with an open collar and no tie, and dirty old slacks. This was Sandy, Susan's boy friend; he was big and heavy, with light red hair.

"Hello," said Susan.

"Hello, Sandy," said Margaret. "When do you go back to college?"

"On September 25th," he said, "in three more weeks. Have you got that new American book? I asked for it in the middle of August." Margaret went to the other desk where the list of new books was.

"Are you coming out this evening?" asked Sandy.

"I must work late tonight because Ann's away ill," said Susan. "I finish at seven o'clock."

Before Sandy answered, Mr Day came out of his office with the young policewoman.

"Young woman," he said to Susan, "please give more time to these people who are waiting, and less to this young man here." Susan was very angry, but she could say nothing. Mr Day spoke to Margaret, "The police have sent us a photograph of the train thief. Look at his picture and read what's under it. Now, Margaret, please put this photograph in the glass case at the door of the library, so that people can see it."

As Mr Day was talking, somebody in the line of people near the desk suddenly ran to the door. Mary, the young policewoman, shouted, "That's the man! That's the man in the photograph!"

"Sandy!" shouted Susan, "that's the man!"

Sandy dropped his books, ran after the man, and arrived at the door before the man did. Sandy stood in front of the door with his arms out. The man hit Sandy once on the chin, and Sandy fell suddenly to the floor. The thief could not open the door because Sandy lay there, and he was too heavy. The man could not pull him away. He looked quickly round the library and saw an open window. He pushed past the people, ran past the desk and down the line of bookcases to the window.

"He's hit Sandy!" shouted Susan. But little Mr Day did not say a word. He ran down the library after the thief, and pulled him back from the open window at the end of the room. Mary, the policewoman, ran behind the bookcases to the window and shut it. At the same time, the thief threw Mr Day to the floor. Mr Day put his arms round the thief's legs. One of the thief's boots hit him in the face, but Mr Day still held on, and pulled the thief to the floor with him. The thief suddenly got away, and when he stood up again, there was a knife in his hand.

"Oh!" said everybody in the library when they saw the knife. Mr Day now had his back to the window. The thief came slowly up to him with his knife. Nobody spoke. Suddenly, before Mr Day could get away, the man's knife-hand flew towards the librarian and cut him badly down the arm. The thief drove him back, away from the window, and then suddenly pushed a high bookcase on top of Mr Day. Now, four other men ran down the library, but the thief was too quick for them. He broke the glass with a heavy book, pushed the window open, and got out into the street.

"Telephone!" shouted the policewoman.

"In Mr Day's office!" said Margaret. Susan was pulling Sandy to his feet.

"Who hit me? Who hit me?" he was saying. At the end of the library, books lay everywhere. The four men found Mr Day under the heavy bookcase. Blood was running from his arm and from his nose.

"I think his nose is broken," said one man. They quickly pushed the books away from him.

"Wait here and don't worry," one said. "We've telephoned the hospital, and the doctor's coming."

Sandy came up to them; Susan was holding his arm. When Sandy saw the blood on Mr Day's clothes, he fainted.

Three minutes later a detective arrived.

"Did anybody see the man in this photograph?" he asked the people. "And what's happened to these two men?" People told the detective about the man who knocked Mr Day down and stabbed him with his knife.

"Thank you, Mr Day," said the detective to the little man who lay on the floor with hundreds of his books round him. "The doctor's coming now."

Then the detective looked at Sandy. "Who's this?" he asked.

"That's Sandy," said Margaret coldly. "The thief hit him once, and when he saw the blood, he fainted."

"That's not kind," said Susan.

"But it's true," said Margaret. "Mr Day's the best man here, and we were wrong about him, Susan."

"I think we were," said Susan quietly. "I'm sorry I spoke badly about him this morning. That knife! Wasn't it awful? I'm going with him to the hospital."

When Sandy opened his eyes he said, "Where's Susan?"

"Gone to the hospital with Mr Day. He's lost a lot of blood," said Margaret.

"I'm going to the hospital too," said Sandy, with his hand to his chin. "Perhaps I can give him some of my blood."

"I don't think so," said Margaret.

The next day, Susan and Sandy were walking through the glass doors of the hospital. Sandy was holding a bag of fruit in one hand and a camera in the other.

"May we see Mr Day?" said Susan to the nurse who was sitting in the office near the door.

"Up the stairs and then to the left," said the nurse.

The two young people stood at the side of Mr Day's bed. Sandy put the bag of fruit down on the small table. "This is a present from us," he said. "You're looking much better now."

"Yes, I am, thank you," said Mr Day, who was sitting up in bed. "I'm going home on Tuesday. Please sit down for a minute and talk."

First they talked about the library, then about the thief who hit Mr Day and ran away.

"Have the police found him yet?" asked Mr Day.

"No," said Susan, "but they think that he's somewhere here still, perhaps only a mile or two away."

"And when are you going back to college, young man?" asked Mr Day.

"In two weeks' time," said Sandy. "I must read three more books from your library before I go back, and write notes on them."

"Are you going to do that this afternoon?"

"No, not this afternoon," said Susan. "He doesn't work on Sunday afternoons, do you Sandy? We are going for a walk."

A bell rang.

"You must go now," said Mr Day. "Thank you again for the present. Good-bye, Susan. Good-bye, Sandy."

They left the hospital and walked down the street past the line of shops.

"Wait here for a minute," said Sandy. "I'm going to take a photograph of you."

"Where do you want me to stand?" asked Susan.

"There," said Sandy, "near that shop window with the fur coats in it. Now, put one hand in your pocket. That's right. Now look to the left, and look happy." Sandy looked through the little window of his camera. "That's very pretty."

He was just going to take the photograph when two men walked in front of him. Sandy waited, and then looked up and down the street. This time nobody was near, so he put the camera to his eye again. "Ready?" he said to Susan. A car stopped behind him, and things happened suddenly. Two men ran up, and one of them threw something heavy at the window of the shop. Broken glass fell into the street. Sandy pushed the button of his camera. The other man climbed through the broken window and then ran quickly to the car with his arms full of fur coats. The first man was helping him. Twice they ran from the shop to the car until the window was empty and the car was full of expensive fur coats. Sandy put his camera to his eye and took two more photographs, one of the window and one of the car. One of the men saw him and shouted to the other, "He's taking photographs of us!" And they ran towards Sandy.

"Get that camera!" said the other man.

"Run, Sandy!" shouted Susan. "Police! Police!"

"Police?" said the first man. "Quick! Into the car!"

"But the camera!"

Sandy was running up the street as fast as he could, his camera in his hands.

"Police!" shouted Susan again.

This time there was a policeman. He was running down the street in his heavy boots when the car drove quickly away.

Susan ran up to him. "Two men," she said, "broke that window and took the fur coats. Then they got in their car and drove away."

"Did you see the number of the car?" asked the policeman.

"Yes, it was OXE 702, an old black car."

Sandy came back. "Did you see those two men?" asked the policeman.

"Yes, I saw them," said Sandy, "and I took their photographs."

"What?"

"I took three photographs."

Then a police car stopped and a detective got out. The policeman told him the story of the broken shop window and the fur coats.

"What was the number of the car?" asked the detective.

"OXE 702," said the policeman.

"Did you see it?" asked the detective.

"No, but this young woman did."

"What did the men look like?" asked the detective.

"This young man took some photographs."

The detective looked at Sandy. "I know you," he said. "Somebody hit you in the library last week."

"That's right," said Sandy.

"These photographs. Are they in colour or in black-and-white?"

"Black-and-white," said Sandy.

"Which photographer do you take your films to?"

"I don't," said Sandy, "I do them myself. I've got the equipment at home."

"Where's your home?"

"In Wood Road, about two miles away."

"Quick!" said the detective. "Into the car!" Then he spoke to the policeman. "Telephone the police station, and give them the number of the car. Then come back here and wait for the others. Look round the shop, too, but telephone first. You, too, Miss. Into the car."

In five minutes they stopped in front of Sandy's house. "You wait in the car, Miss," said the detective. "Here's some paper. Please write down what you saw at the shop." Sandy was running to the side door of his house, and the detective ran after him. Through the kitchen they went, up the stairs and into the bathroom.

"Who's that? What's happening?" shouted Sandy's mother.

"Don't worry, Mother," Sandy shouted back. "There's a detective in here with me. Don't open the door. We're working on a film."

Sandy opened his camera and took out the film. "Give me that bottle, the big one," he said to the detective. But the room was black and the detective could see nothing.

"You must do it," said the detective. "I don't know where things are."

"Very well," said Sandy, and with careful fingers he put the film into the first basin.

At the same time, fifteen miles away, a police car stopped an old black car with the number OXE 702. There were three men in it, but no fur coats. The police took the three men to the police station.

"Now," said Sandy, "please open the door."

"Have you finished?" asked the detective.

"Half finished," said Sandy.

"Is there a telephone here?"

"Yes, in the living-room. Ask my mother. I must close the door again now. Please don't open it again."

The detective telephoned the police station. "We've got three men," said the man at the station, "but there were no coats with them. The men say that they've been in a hotel in town today. They say they haven't been near the shop. Perhaps the girl's wrong about the number of the car. We can't hold these men."

"Hold them for half an hour. Wait for these photographs."

"Very well, but only half an hour," said the man at the station.

The detective went upstairs and knocked at the bathroom door. "Have you finished?" he asked.

"I've just finished," said Sandy. "I'm coming out now." And there was Sandy, with two wet photographs in his hand.

"Have you got a picture of the car?" said the detective.

"No," said Sandy, "that one's no good. I took it looking into the sun. But look at these." The detective looked at the two photographs very carefully.

"Beautiful!" he said. "Into the car!"

They were driving at full speed to the police station when Susan said, "May I see the pictures, please?"

"Be careful with them," said Sandy, "they're still wet."

She looked first at one, and then at the other. "Look at this," she said suddenly. "Do you see this man? He's the man who came into the library and hit Mr Day."

"He hit me too, don't forget," said Sandy. "Let me look. Yes, that's the man."

"Is he the man carrying the coats in this picture?" asked the detective.

"No," said Susan, "he's in this first photograph. There, just behind me. He's throwing something at the shop window. And that's a good picture of me too, isn't it?" The detective laughed.

The car arrived at the police station. "Are the men still here?" asked the detective.

"Yes," said the man at the desk. "Two of them are in there, and the third one's in the Interview Room."

"Hold those two men," said the detective. "Give me the photographs, and wait here," he said to Sandy and Susan. Then he knocked on the door of the Interview Room . . .

And that is the end of the story. The police found the thief, and two others as well. Mr Day got better and went back to his work in the public library. Sandy went back to college. Before he went he gave Susan a big photograph which shows her in front of the fur shop with the window broken and two men with their arms full of fur coats. She has put the picture on the table in her bedroom. Margaret has been three times to the cinema with Mr Day.

But the police have still not found those fur coats.

The food of love

The time was ten minutes to nine. Hundreds of boys and girls were walking down the road to the big school. Some were getting out of buses and others were riding their bicycles. In their hands or on their backs were bags full of books. The younger boys and girls, who were about twelve years old, were wearing bright new school clothes because the school year was just starting. It was a Tuesday morning in the middle of September, and the second day of school.

Ben Smith got out of his car behind the school and saw his friend, Peter Walker, the music teacher. Peter waited for him, and they went through the big door of the school.

"Ben," said Peter, "do you know that boy over there?"

"Where?" said Ben.

"The one with dark hair, near the secretary's office," said Peter.

"Yes, I know him. I don't teach him, but I know him. I didn't know he was coming to this school. Now, what's his name? Brian something? I've forgotten."

"Yes, Brian York," said the other teacher. "And he's just started at this school."

"I know his family has just bought a house on Green Road," said Ben.

"His father says that he's a very good pianist," said Peter. "He says he's a beautiful player."

"Have you heard this young man?" asked Ben.

"No," said the music teacher. "I'm very busy. I can't listen to him for a week or two. Look, tell me about your daughter, Penny. Is she still playing her violin well?"

"Oh, yes, she practises a lot, and she's getting better."

"Good," said Peter. "I want to talk to you about her for a minute."

"At lunch-time," said Ben. "I must go and teach now."

"Have you had a good day, Ben?" asked his wife that evening, when he arrived home. "Has Penny come with you?"

"Yes, I've had a good day," said Ben, "and no, Penny hasn't come with me."

"She usually comes with you," said June.

"Not this week," said Ben. "She walks now. She walks home down Green Road."

"I don't understand it," said June. "Do you want a cup of tea now?"

Fifteen minutes later Penny arrived. She put her books down on a chair.

"Why do you walk home now, Penny?" asked her mother.

"I was talking to Mr Walker today," said Ben quickly, "about your violin."

"I know. I'm not going to play," said Penny.

"Play what? Play when?" asked June.

"There's going to be a musical evening at the school, for parents and friends," explained Ben. "Peter Walker told me at lunch-time. Penny's going to play."

"That's very good," said June. "Perhaps we can ask the Storys to come with us. They like music."

"No, it's not good!" said Penny. "And I'm not going to play!"

"But why not?" asked Ben.

"Because Mr Walker says he's going to play the piano for me," said Penny, "and I don't want that. He doesn't play well. Oh, I can't explain!" And Penny ran upstairs to her bedroom.

"Do you want your tea?" shouted June.

"No!" Penny shouted back.

"Oh, dear!" said June. "Isn't she angry, the silly girl. What are we going to do?"

"Leave her," said Ben. "I have an idea." He looked at his wife and laughed.

"I don't understand," said June.

On Wednesday afternoon at four o'clock, when the boys and girls were walking and running and riding home at the end of the day, Ben Smith was waiting with his car in front of the school. He carefully watched the bigger boys and finally saw the one he was looking for.

He opened the left-hand door of his car and said, "Hello, Brian, I'm going back to my house down Green Road today. Perhaps I can take you home."

"Oh," said Brian, "hello, Mr Smith. Thank you, but I think . . . you see, I must . . ."

"Come on," said Ben. "Get in the car." So Brian got in, and sat uncomfortably and quietly in Ben Smith's little car. He did not understand what was happening. Ben was talking about the school and the teachers. He was still talking when they went past Brian's house.

"Thank you, Mr Smith," Brian said. "We have gone past my . . ." But Ben did not stop, and talked and talked. Brian could say nothing, just yes and no. Suddenly Ben stopped in front of his house.

"Here we are, young man," he said. "You get out here."

"But this isn't my home, this is your house," said Brian.

"Well!" said Ben, "so it is! I forgot I was taking you home. But come in for just a minute. Then you can go home."

"But Mr Smith," said Brian, "I can easily walk home from here." Ben took the young man by the arm to the house, and pushed him through the door.

"June!" he shouted, "there's a young man here. Give him a drink of tea or something."

"A young man? What young man?" said June from upstairs. She came down, looked at Ben but did not speak to him. When she saw Brian she said, "Oh, good afternoon. Your parents have just bought the new house on Green Road, isn't that right? Now you go to Penny's school, don't you? Come and sit down."

"No, don't sit down here," said Ben. "Go into the other room for just a minute. In there, the room where the piano is." And Ben shut the door of the living-room behind Brian.

"Ben," said his wife, "come here! Please tell me what's happening. Why have you brought that young man here, and why have you put him in the living-room? I don't understand."

Ben did not answer her, but only said, "Here's Penny. Now we can have tea."

"Well," said June, "perhaps Penny understands what's happening." But Penny was not very happy, and said nothing to her mother.

"What's wrong with you?" asked June.

"Somebody didn't come," she said, and threw her books on a chair.

"Everybody is very, very stupid this afternoon," said June. "I'm going to get very angry in a minute."

"Be quiet," said Ben, "and listen."

Suddenly somebody was playing the piano in the living-room. Ben Smith, his wife and his daughter stood quietly in the kitchen, and listened. The music went on and on. They all listened without a word. Finally it stopped.

"That was beautiful," said June.

"But who is it?" asked Penny. "Is it on television?"

"Go and look," said Ben. Penny opened the door and saw Brian, who was looking through the books of music on top of the piano. Her face went very red. She pushed the door shut behind her.

"How did you get here?" she asked in a quiet voice.

"Your father brought me in his car."

"What!"

"He said he was going to take me home, but he brought me here."

"Is that why you didn't wait for me at the end of Green Road?" asked Penny.

"Yes," said Brian. "What could I do?"

"Don't worry about that," said Penny. "Were you playing the piano just now?"

"Yes."

"You played beautifully. Can you play this piece?" She took a music book from the top of the piano, and opened the pages.

"This top line's for the violin," said Brian. "I can play the piano part."

"Then wait a minute," said Penny. She took her violin case from behind a chair and took out the violin.

"So you play the violin?" asked Brian.

"Yes."

"Now I understand, I think," said Brian.

Penny pointed to the page of music open on the piano. "You start there," she said, "and I come in here. Are you ready?"

Ben and June sat in the kitchen and listened to the violin and piano music from the living-room.

"Did you know he could play the piano?" asked June.

"Peter Walker told me," said Ben, "but I didn't know he played as well as this."

"And did you know that Penny and this boy were friends?"

"I saw her with him after school at the end of Green Road. That was on Monday. That's why she has walked home this week."

The music stopped. Penny and Brian came out of the living-room.

"Where are you going now? Stay and have some supper with us," said Ben.

"No," said Penny, "Brian must go home now. I'm going to walk to the end of the road with him. Just for five minutes."

"Are you going to play at the musical evening at school?" asked Ben.

"Yes," said Penny, "but not with Mr Walker. Please tell him to-morrow I'm going to play the violin and Brian's going to play the piano for me." And the two young people went out.

"Suddenly I am very tired and hungry," said Ben. "Can we have some supper now?"

"But I don't quite understand . . ." began June.

Games at the party

The clock on Tony Cook's desk said five o'clock. He picked up the telephone and spoke to his secretary.

"Myra," he said, "I'm going home now. The supper's at eight o'clock, and I must be at the New York restaurant at half past seven. I must be there before the boss."

"Very well, Mr Cook," said his secretary, "and don't forget your ticket this evening. Mr London told me today I must be sure that everybody has got a ticket when they come in."

"Thank you, Myra," said Tony Cook. "I've got the ticket safe in my wallet."

At half past five the offices of the company were empty. Everybody was getting ready for the supper and the party later in the evening.

What is this party for? Tony Cook works for Mr London, and his company makes chairs and tables. Only a mile away is another company which makes chairs and tables too. Mr London's company is bigger, and it is going to buy the smaller company. So the people who work in the offices of both companies are all going to a party at the New York restaurant. The supper is for sixty-five people.

Myra went to the hairdresser when she left the office. Then she went home, had a bath and put on her best clothes. All the secretaries and the other girls who worked in the office were going to wear their best clothes. Myra arrived at the restaurant at half past seven. Mr Cook was standing at the door, very smart in his black evening clothes.

"Ah, Myra," he said when he saw her, "you've come very early. Just give me a hand. When the people come, I want you to stand here at the door and take their tickets. I must go and see that the room's ready, and the flowers too."

At a quarter to eight the first people arrived. Myra did not know them because they were from the other company, but they all had their tickets. Then the others came, office girls from her company, and the older men who worked there too. They were all happy, and very noisy. At five to eight a lot of people from the other company all came through the doors together.

Mr Cook came out of the supper-room.

"Have you seen all the tickets, Myra?" he asked.

Before Myra could answer, Mr London arrived, with the boss of the other company, and their wives. Then everybody went into the supper-room, and supper started.

It was not a very comfortable supper. The people from one company sat at one side of the room, and the people from the other company sat on the other side. Mr London and the boss of the other company sat at the top table, but they did not speak much, or laugh. And because the bosses were quiet, everybody was quiet. You could hear the knives and forks and glasses, and that was all. People got more and more uncomfortable, and drank more wine. Finally, when the fruit was on the table, and the coffee, Mr London stood up.

He spoke for half an hour about the two companies, about his friend, the boss of the other company, about tables and chairs, and about money and wages. But he did not speak well, and some people who were sitting at the ends of the tables could not hear him. Finally he sat down, and the boss of the other company stood up. He spoke badly, too; sometimes he forgot what he was going to say and when he sat down everybody was very tired. The room was quiet.

Then suddenly a man, who was sitting at the end of one of the tables, stood up. He had a big red face, and his hair fell in front of his eyes. He pushed his hair back with one hand and took a big glass of wine in the other.

"Drink with me!" he shouted. "Drink with me to both the companies!"

Everybody stood up.

"To the companies!" shouted the man.

"To our companies!" everybody said.

"To tables and chairs!" he shouted. "And empty your glasses!"

Sixty-five empty glasses rang on the table.

"Is everybody happy?" shouted the man with the big red face.

"Yes!" they all answered.

"Then come and dance!"

The music started. He took the hand of the girl who was sitting next to

c

him, and danced down the room with her. "Come on, everybody! Dance! On to the floor!"

In one minute all the people in the room were dancing. The seats were empty; the dance floor was full.

"This is better," said Myra, who was dancing with Tony Cook. "The supper was horrible."

"I thought the food was quite good," said Tony Cook.

"Oh, the food was good," said Myra, "but when Mr London and that other man were talking it was horrible."

"It's better now," said Tony Cook. "I'm glad that man from the other company is here tonight."

"Who?"

"The man with the red face."

"Oh, yes," said Myra. "Look! Here he is again. Oh, look!"

The man with the big red face was running into the room from the kitchen of the restaurant. In his hands were six big bottles of wine.

"Drink, my friends!" he shouted. "There's some more wine here." And the glasses were all full again.

Mr London was dancing with his wife.

"I like parties," said Mrs London, "when everybody is so happy."

The man with the red face came behind Mr London.

"Excuse me," he said, and took Mrs London in his arms and danced down the room with her. His mouth was red with wine. Mr London looked round him.

"Well!" he said to himself. But the next minute Mr London was dancing with Myra, Tony Cook's secretary.

So the evening went on. There was always wine in bottles on the table, and in the glasses. The man with the red face laughed and drank more and more. His face got redder and redder.

"Stop the music!" he shouted. "We're going to play a game."

"What game?" they all asked.

"Bring six chairs!" he said. "Six chairs. And I want twelve people." He put the chairs on the floor in two lines. "Six people on those three chairs, and six on the others. Now!" he went on, "you're in a bus, and the bus is full of people. Here are twelve newspapers, but you see the pages are in the wrong order. You must put them in the right order. Don't fall off the chairs. Are you ready? Go!"

What a mess of newspapers on the floor! Pages of newspapers flew about the room. Everybody shouted and laughed. Mr London, who was one of the twelve people, suddenly fell from his chair.

"Get up! Get up!" shouted the man with the big red face.

"We've finished!" shouted the six people on the other three chairs.

"More wine, more wine!" shouted the man. "We must drink to the people who finished first!" And he quickly emptied his glass. "Now we're going to have another game!"

"Good!" shouted Mr London. "What game's this?"

The man pushed his red face very near to Mr London, put his hands on the collar of his coat, and said, "When you put a woman's hair in wine, it turns white, in just one minute."

"It's not true," said Mr London.

"It is true," said the man, "and I'm going to show you." He drank more wine out of his glass.

"It's silly," said Mr London.

"Oh, no," said the man. "Come round this end of the table, everybody." He pushed glasses, plates, knives and forks from the end of the table, and took a bottle of wine which was nearly full.

"Now I want a woman's hair," he said. "A black one is best." He saw Myra, who was standing near the table, and he quickly pulled a hair out of her head.

"Oh!" said Myra.

The man put some wine from the bottle on to the table.

"Now," he said, "you are going to see this black hair turn white when I put it in this wine."

"I can't see the hair," said the boss of the other company.

"Come near!" said the man. "Come right up to the table! You are too high, Mr London, put your head down here. Now, do you all see the hair?" And he held the hair in the fingers of both hands.

"Yes," they said. "We can see."

"Watch carefully," said the man, and he slowly put the hair in the pool of wine on the table. "Do you see it?"

"No," said somebody. Twenty people were standing round, with their faces near the table. Suddenly the man with the red face threw his hands down into the pool of wine!

"Oh!" said everybody. The twenty people stood up quickly. Their faces were wet with wine. Everybody was laughing. The man with the big red face took up his wine glass again, but before he could drink he suddenly fell on to the table. Glasses and plates broke on the floor.

Tony Cook lifted the man's head from the pool of wine. His eyes were shut and his mouth open. Then the man fell slowly to the floor and lay on his back on the carpet.

"Is he ill?" asked Myra.

"I don't think he's ill," said Tony Cook, "but he has drunk a lot of wine. Three bottles, I think."

"Now," said Mr London to the boss of the other company, "he's going to sleep for a long time. You must take him home."

"Why must I take him home?" asked the other man.

"He's in your company, isn't he?" asked Mr London.

"No, he's not. I thought he was in your company," said the other man. They were both quiet for a minute. Everybody came and looked at the man on the floor. He lay there with his eyes shut and his mouth open. Nobody knew him. Nobody knew his name.

"Well," said Mr London to Tony Cook, "you looked at the tickets at the door. You said he could come in. You take him home. And see me tomorrow in my office."

"Oh, dear," said Tony Cook to himself. "What can I do?'"

People slowly went out of the room, took their coats and walked out of the restaurant.

The manager of the restaurant came up to Tony Cook.

"What can I do with him?" asked Tony.

"You go home," said the manager. "Don't worry. He can stay here. You go home. You look ill yourself. This red Spanish wine is very strong." So Tony Cook went out slowly. He held his head in his hands and walked home.

The manager took a glass of water and threw it in the man's face. The man suddenly sat up.

"Hello, Tom," said the manager, "was it a good party tonight?"

"It was a beautiful party," said the man with the big red face, "better than the one last week."

Snow in the mountains

The two cars stopped in the car park under the trees.

"Here they are," said the manager. He watched from the front door of the hotel as five people got out of the two cars and looked round them. The manager walked out and spoke to the three men and two women who were taking a lot of camera equipment out of the boots of the cars.

"Good evening," he said. "I'm glad you have arrived so early. Come, I'll show you to your rooms. You can leave that equipment downstairs. George will take it to your rooms after supper. Good evening," he said to the two women. "Supper will be at seven o'clock. Come inside; it's cold out here." As he went back into his office he shouted, "George! Please carry these cases upstairs. Rooms eight, ten, and eleven. Here are the keys."

It was early in the year. At half past six the sun was going down, and the sky over the tops of the mountains was angry with dark red clouds. The woods on the sides of the mountains were black and quiet.

The two women sat by the window of the downstairs room, and looked out.

"Beautiful," said one of them.

"I'm very glad we came with them," said the other. "I think this is the best time of the year in these mountains, don't you, Mary?"

"Oh, yes," said Mary. "We came up here for a week last year, Francis and I. We climbed all over these mountains. That was why Bill and Francis and Tom came up here this time."

The manager came in.

"I hope you'll be comfortable," he said. "It's quiet here in April, you know. You are the only people here. So you're going to take photographs?" he asked, and he looked at the equipment lying in a corner of the room.

"Yes," said Mary, "we've come from London, and our husbands work in television. Oh, you tell him, Jane. You know all about it."

"You see," said Jane, "they're making a television film from a story in a book, and some of it happens in a country of forests and mountains. So we're going to take some film tomorrow. Later, perhaps, the actors will be coming."

"Later this week?"

"Oh, no. I think in June or July."

The three men came in and they all went into the restaurant.

"Are you ready for tomorrow?" asked Francis, and looked at the two women. "We must be up early, you know. We must get up to the snow before the middle of the day."

"Yes," said Bill, who was Jane's husband, "we must get the cameras up there before the sky gets cloudy."

"So what time must we start?" asked Mary.

"Five o'clock," said Tom, and laughed.

"No!" said Mary.

"Well, we must be away from here before half past seven," said Tom.

"Or seven o'clock," said Bill.

"Breakfast at half past six?" Francis asked the manager of the hotel.

"Oh, yes," said the manager, "it will be ready for you then."

"So," said Tom, "Bill and I will put the film in the cameras tonight."

"And are you going to climb the mountain with us tomorrow?" Francis asked the two wives.

"That's a silly question," said Mary. "That's why we've come. We're not going to sit here all day and wait for you."

"Good," said Bill. "Then early bed for everybody. Tomorrow will be a hard day."

But Jane did not go with the others in the morning because she was ill in the middle of the night.

"What's wrong?" asked Bill, when Jane switched on the light.

"It's my head," said Jane, "and my eyes."

"Can I get you anything?" asked Bill. "Do you want a doctor?" He looked at the clock by the bed. The time was half past two.

"Oh, no," said Jane. "I'm not as ill as that. Just give me my hand-bag. It's there on the chair. I think I've got something there."

Bill found the little brown bottle, and brought his wife a glass of water too.

"Don't worry," said Jane. "I'll be fine. Go to sleep."

Bill's alarm clock rang at half past six. He opened his eyes. His wife was still sleeping, but she looked ill and her face was white. He washed, put his clothes on quietly, and went downstairs. The other three were at breakfast.

"Hello, Bill," said Francis. "Where's Jane?"

"She was ill in the small hours, at about two o'clock," said Bill. "She was sleeping when I came down."

"I'll go up," said Mary, "and see if she's better now." She drank her coffee and went upstairs. She was ready for the day, in her heavy boots and warm clothes.

Bill ate his breakfast.

"I don't think she can go with us," he said. "It'll be a hard long day on those mountains."

"That's true," said Tom, "but will you stay here with her?"

Then Mary came downstairs again.

"She's a little better now," she said, "but she's going to stay in bed this morning. I'll take her breakfast to her, and I think I'll stay here with her today."

"Oh, no," said Bill, "I don't think Jane wants that." And he went upstairs with Mary.

"You must all go," said Jane from her bed, "all four of you. Be sensible, please. I'll stay in bed this morning and get up when I'm better. Go on, Mary. Leave the breakfast here. I'll be fine. I'll sleep again soon and get up later. Oh! my head!"

So, when the sun came up from behind the mountains the four people put their cameras into one car, and drove to the highest mountain with snow on top of it. As the morning went on, Jane slept and read a book and slept again.

The others drove to the end of the road, and took their cameras out of the boot of the car.

"This is where we get out and walk," said Tom. "Is everybody ready?" He went first and carried the biggest camera. For half an hour they climbed through trees up a little narrow road, and then they found themselves on the open side of the mountain. They looked down over the tops of the trees, and could see the road from the hotel.

Tom was still in front.

"Too fast?" he asked.

"Too fast, Mary?" asked Francis.

"No," she said, "I can walk like this all day."

"We're all fine, Tom," shouted Bill. "When we get up near the snow we'll stop for a drink. Francis, give me the other camera. I can carry it now."

"And give me those heavy binoculars," said Mary.

The sun climbed higher into the beautiful blue sky. In the trees it was cold, but up on the side of the mountain the sun was hot. Now they saw more and more of the country round them. They were going more slowly now, as they went higher up the mountain. The ground under their feet was difficult, and a little dangerous too. Tom still went carefully in front. The others looked up and saw the bottoms of his heavy boots as he went up and up the side of the mountain.

"We're near the snow now," said Bill, who was behind the others. They said nothing, but climbed slowly on. The cameras were very heavy now, as well as the bags of food and film, and the binoculars.

Suddenly Tom sat down and waited for the others.

"I want a drink," he said. Tom did not talk much, but he was a very good climber, and he knew more than the others about television films too.

Mary opened the bag which Francis was carrying, and gave everybody a drink of coffee. They ate a little of their food too. They looked round them. The top of the mountain was near. The white snow lay in the sun. Here and there were pieces of dark ground. Behind, the sky was blue.

"This is what we want for the first pieces of film," said Tom. "Put the camera up here, Bill." When the camera was ready, Bill found the key, which was like the key of a clock, put it in the camera, and turned it.

"Now," said Tom, "go from the sky over there, past the top of the mountain, down the snow on this side to the trees down there."

"Ready," said Bill, and started the camera. The others watched him.

"Good, stop it there," said Tom. "Now for the second one, Bill."

Bill had his eye to the window in the back of the camera.

"Start at the top of the mountain over there, and . . ."

"Wait!" shouted Bill. "Do you see that?"

"What?" said the others.

"There, in the sky, to the left of that mountain. Two of them!"

Mary was looking through the binoculars. "Yes!" she said. "Do you see, Francis? Those two birds!"

High in the morning sky two big grey and brown birds were flying slowly round. They came nearer and nearer to the four people who were standing with their cameras near the top of the mountain, in the warm April sun.

"What are they?" asked Mary. They were all looking up into the blue sky. "You know about birds," she said to Bill. "What are they?"

"I thought I knew the names of all the birds in these mountains," said Bill, "but these are too big. Look at them!"

The pair of birds beat their wings slowly over the heads of the four people, and flew round and round.

"They are looking at us," said Tom. "Perhaps they're hungry."

Then one bird called to the other and they suddenly went down on the other side of the mountain.

"Well, that's that," said Tom. "Now we must take that second piece of film."

But Bill was packing the camera and its equipment into its bag.

"What are you doing?" said Tom. "We haven't finished with the camera here."

"I'm going after those birds," said Bill. "Perhaps we shall never see them again. I think they went down just on the other side of the mountain. With this equipment we can take some very good film of them."

"But they're miles away now," said Mary.

"I don't think so," said Bill. "Look, Tom, I'll leave the other camera with you and I'll come back to you here."

"But it's very dangerous," said Tom. "The ground from here to the top is rough. And you're carrying that heavy camera bag. No, I don't like it."

"I'll go with him," said Francis suddenly. "We'll be very careful, Tom, and we'll be back here in an hour, no more."

Tom thought for a minute, and then said, "I'll go with Bill. You stay here, Francis, with Mary, and take the film we want with the other camera."

"When will you be back?" asked Francis.

"In no more than an hour," said Tom. "Give me the camera," he said to Bill. "You go in front."

The other two watched. Slowly, Bill and Tom climbed the dangerous side of the mountain up to the top. Mary saw the two climbers, very small now, black on the white snow. In twenty minutes they were standing together at the top. Then they were gone down the other side.

"Will they be safe?" asked Mary.

"Oh, yes," said Francis. "Tom knows what he's doing. Come on, Mary, we'll make a good job of the film we take from here. Look, the sun is just right on those trees now."

The day outside was sunny and warm. Jane was reading her book when the manager's wife brought her a drink of coffee and the newspaper.

"Shall I bring your lunch up to your room?" asked the manager's wife.

"No, thank you," said Jane. "I think I'll get up at about twelve o'clock. It's a beautiful day, isn't it? And I'm much better now."

"I'll give you your lunch at about half past twelve," said the manager's wife.

"Please just a little lunch," said Jane. "I'm not very hungry."

"Some fish?"

"That will be very nice. Then I'll sit in the garden in the sun."

But when Jane was eating her piece of fish in the lunch-room, the sun went in. She looked out of the window and saw that the sky was cloudy. She could not see the top of the mountain with the snow on it, and it was colder in the hotel now.

On the mountain, Francis took the last piece of film and put the camera away in its bag. Mary helped him, and packed away the other equipment. The sky was whiter now.

"The best of the day has gone," said Francis, who was sitting down on the cold ground and drinking a second cup of coffee.

"Have they been away an hour, the other two?" asked Mary.

"An hour and a half," said Francis.

"An hour and a half!"

"A little more than that," Francis said. "But don't worry. Tom will be safe. He'll look after Bill. As I said, he knows what he's doing."

"But why haven't they come back?" said Mary. "Is there anything we can do?"

They both looked up to the top of the mountain, and both saw, at the same time, the two big grey and brown birds. High over the mountain-top they flew. Then, right on the top of the mountain stood a man.

"Here they come," said Francis. "I said don't worry."

But only one man was coming. And he was coming fast down the dangerous side of the mountain. Sometimes he was nearly running.

"Who is it? Can you see?" said Mary.

"It's Tom," said Francis. "Something's wrong. Wait here. I'll go and meet him."

But Mary followed Francis and shouted, "Be careful, Tom!" Because Tom was now running down the side of the mountain. When they all met, Tom could not speak.

"Quick!" said Francis. "Give him a drink, Mary."

Tom put the cup to his mouth. His hands were shaking, and the cup hit his teeth. Some of the hot coffee went down the front of his coat.

"There's been an accident," he said finally. "Bill, he's in trouble. He..."

"Tell us slowly, Tom," said Mary. "Come here and sit down."

"There's no time for that," said Tom. "He's lying there on the other side of the mountain."

"What happened?"

"He went after those birds," said Tom. "He was trying to get a photograph. I told him it was dangerous, but he went on down. There was ice there. Then those two birds got angry, and flew near his head. I shouted to him. Suddenly he fell. I couldn't get to him quickly so I came back here. I think he's broken a leg."

The others were quiet for a minute.

"I'll go to him," said Francis. "Where is he?"

"No," said Tom. "We must think about this. Who knows where we are now?"

"Jane knows we're on this mountain," said Mary. "But she won't worry about us before it gets dark. And she's ill."

"So somebody must go down now," said Tom. "I'll go back to Bill. You, Francis and Mary, get down this mountain as quickly as you can. Get to the car, go to the nearest house and telephone the police."

"Have you got the key of the car?" said Mary.

"Here it is," said Tom, and pulled the key out of his pocket. "Give me all the food, and all the warm clothes, yes, your coats too."

Mary and Francis took off their warm coats.

"I'll take that scarf, too, Mary," said Tom. "You'll be down at the car in two hours. Where's the coffee?"

"We've drunk it all," said Mary.

"Oh, dear," said Tom, "Bill will want a hot drink."

Two minutes later, Francis and Mary were climbing down the mountain, and Tom was climbing back up with his heavy bag of food and warm clothes.

In the hotel it was half past seven in the evening. Supper for five people was waiting. Jane was reading the newspaper:

BIRDS TAKE CAT

Yesterday, two big birds flew into the garden of a house in Grey Road, and flew away with Mr and Mrs Short's cat. Nobody knows what these birds are and nobody has seen them again. . . .

Jane looked out of the window. It was very dark outside, and it was raining.

"It's often like this at this time of the year," said the manager. "In the morning the weather is beautiful and sunny. Then it gets cloudy in the afternoon, and after that there's heavy rain. On the mountains it's snowing now, I'm sure. When are your people coming back?"

"They said six o'clock," said Jane. "They're very late."

"That's true," said the manager of the hotel, "but you have your supper now. We can keep the other food hot. They'll be here later. Don't worry."

Francis and Mary were half-way down to their car when Tom found Bill again on the other side of the mountain. Tom climbed down carefully over the ice, with his heavy bag. Then, suddenly, the cloudy sky came down on the top of the mountain and Tom could see nothing. He stopped.

"Bill," he called, "I'm coming. Where are you?"

"Over here, to your right," said a quiet voice from the side.

When he started again, Tom nearly fell on the dangerous ice, but he climbed slowly down to where Bill lay. Now, through the cloudy sky, rain was falling, a slow, cold rain.

Bill's broken leg lay under him, and his hands were very cold. There was no drink for him. Tom carefully pulled the broken leg from under Bill.

"Ah!" shouted Bill.

"A little more," said Tom, and now the broken leg lay by the side of the good one. Tom tied the two legs together with pieces of Mary's scarf.

"Now we must wait," thought Tom.

"Where are the others?" asked Bill, his face white.

"They've gone down to the car," said Tom, and he put the warm coats round Bill, and under him too.

"We shall soon see them again," said Bill, with his eyes shut. "Francis will telephone the police, and in an hour or two we shall be away from here."

"That's right," said Tom. "Just lie there and keep still."

He looked at the cloudy, rainy weather round him, and he knew that nobody could find them for a long time, but he did not say this to Bill. He gave him a sandwich, and put another coat on him.

Slowly the dark evening fell on the cold mountain. On the other side, Francis and Mary lost the road down to the car. They found themselves in trees, but there was no road. They walked on slowly through the heavy, cloudy weather. Soon it was late evening. They could not see their hands in front of their faces. They held hands and walked on, but it was no good. Under their feet the ground was wet and dangerous. Heavy drops of water from the black trees fell on their faces. They had no coats.

"We can't go on," said Mary. "It's awful!"

"We must," said Francis. "Think of Bill with his broken leg. We must get help." And he walked on, but unhappily he fell, and hit his face hard on a big tree.

"What have you done?" shouted Mary. "Where are you?"

"Down here," said Francis. "I've hit my nose on this tree." The warm blood was running down his face. "It's no good," he went on, "we must stay here and find the road when morning comes."

They both sat down. The rain fell on Mary's blouse and Francis's shirt.

"It must be raining hard on the mountain too," said Mary.

But she was wrong. Up on the side of the mountain the rain stopped at ten o'clock that evening. The weather got colder and it snowed hard.

Down at the hotel Jane did not know it was snowing up in the mountains. The rain was beating at the hotel windows when she telephoned the police at ten o'clock.

"Are you going to bed?" asked the manager's wife.

"No," said Jane, "I can't sleep. You go to bed, please. I'll sit down here." So Jane sat in the big chair in the downstairs room of the hotel. She opened a book, but she could not see the words. She sat through the long hours with her eyes open, and waited for the day.

It was about four o'clock in the morning when Mary said, "Francis, I think the rain has stopped." She was shaking with cold, and all her clothes were wet. She looked up to the tops of the big trees and could just see the sky.

"Francis!" she said. "We must do something. We must get warm!"

Francis stood up slowly.

"Where are you?" he said, and then he found her hand. It was like ice.

"We must go down through the trees," said Mary. "These trees don't go on for ever."

"Be very careful, and don't go fast," said Francis. They put one hand out in front of them, and started down.

Tom sat in the snow on the mountain-top and waited. The food was all gone. Bill lay by his side, and Tom thought he was sleeping. It was still snowing a little, and ice and snow lay on their coats.

Slowly the sky went from black to grey, and then red. The sun was coming up. Bill's face was hot, and Tom thought that he was very ill.

But Tom could do nothing. Only wait. His tired eyes watched the sky. He put snow in a cup and made it warm with his hands. He put the cup to Bill's mouth, but Bill did not drink. Still Tom watched the sky, and the side of the mountain in front of him.

"Come on, come on, somebody!" he said to himself.

At six o'clock the telephone rang in the hotel. The manager answered it. "No," he said into the telephone, "nobody has come back . . . Yes, an awful night . . . Yes, I'll tell her that . . . Good-bye," and he put the telephone down.

"Is that the police?" asked Jane. She was still sitting in the chair in the downstairs room.

"Yes," said the manager. "Now, don't worry. My wife is making a good hot breakfast for all of us. The police say that a helicopter is going out at seven o'clock, and a party of climbers is ready. But the helicopter is going first. Come, drink this coffee. Everything's going to be fine."

At half past six Francis and Mary came to the end of the wood. They were wet and dirty, hungry and tired, and very cold. There was blood on Francis's face and down the front of his shirt. But now the sun was coming up, and the dark and dangerous time was past.

"Look!" said Francis. In front of them was a country road, rough and full of holes, and the holes were full of water. "Come on!" he shouted. "Run and get warm!" And the two of them ran hand in hand down the dirty road. Finally they came to a better road, with white lines, a broad open road.

"I know this!" shouted Francis. "I know where we are. Up there is the road to the mountain, where we left the car, and down here is the hotel."

"But where are we going now?" asked Mary.

Francis thought for a minute. "To the hotel," he said, "and we'll stop at the first house we see. That's the best thing."

But they never got to the first house. They started down the road. Sometimes they ran. When they were tired they walked. Then they ran again.

"Do you hear?" asked Francis suddenly. They both listened. A car was coming up the road.

"This is better still," said Francis. "Here he comes! Stop him, Mary!"

They both stood in the middle of the road with their hands over their heads. The car stopped quickly. Then they saw it was a police car with two policemen in it.

"What's this?" said the policeman who was driving. "Please get out of the way. This is an emergency. Some people are in trouble on the mountain. We can't stop."

"But we *are* those people," said Mary. "We are *two* of them. The others are still on the top of the mountain."

"Why?" asked the other policeman.

"Because one has broken his leg."

"Where is he?"

"Over the top. On the other side from where we are now."

"When did he break his leg?" asked the driver of the car.

"Yesterday. In the afternoon."

"And where were you when it was snowing?"

"In the trees, there, up the side of the mountain," said Mary, who was standing there and shaking in her wet clothes.

"You went up that mountain with no coats?" asked the other policeman.

"We gave our coats to Tom. He stayed with the man who broke his leg."

"Get in," said the other policeman, and he opened the back door of the car. The driver was speaking through his radio.

"Yes," he was saying, "two of them . . . near the top . . . one has a broken leg. . . . Yes, very difficult. . . . Will you tell the helicopter pilot? . . . Good. . . . Out," he said, and he put the radio telephone back on the shelf under the front window of the car.

The driver then turned the car round and started down the road to the hotel.

"You had a cold night under those trees," said the other policeman. The car was warm inside, and Mary was sleeping.

"Very uncomfortable," said Francis.

The helicopter was flying high over the ground. It was seven o'clock and a fine sunny morning. The sky over the pilot's head was a beautiful blue colour, and under him were the mountains and trees. Snow lay on the mountains, white in the morning sun, and here and there snow lay in the dark trees.

"It snowed a lot," shouted the pilot to his second man.

"Yes, very bad weather," shouted the second man.

The noisy helicopter beat through the cold sunny morning.

"The radio!" shouted the second man, and for two minutes he answered the man on the ground who was talking to him.

"Good," he said to the pilot. "We know now what we're looking for – two men, near the top of that mountain, on our side. They'll be in the snow."

"What's wrong with them?" shouted the pilot. "Why didn't they go down yesterday?"

"One has broken his leg," said the second man.

"More than fifteen hours on the top of that mountain, with a broken leg, in bad weather," shouted the pilot. "We've got some trouble here."

Tom heard the helicopter before he saw it. He was looking at a piece of fur which was lying on the ground near his foot.

"Fur?" he was saying to himself. "Cat fur? Do cats live on the tops of mountains?" And then he heard the helicopter. He stood up and took off his top coat. Then the plane came out of the blue sky high over his head. Tom put the black coat on the white snow. He was taking off his other coat when he saw that the helicopter pilot was not flying on.

"He's seen me!" said Tom to himself. "Bill! Bill! They've come!"

"Francis . . . and Mary . . . and Jane," said Bill in a quiet voice. He opened his eyes and saw nobody.

"They've come just in time," said Tom to himself. "He's very ill."

The helicopter beat the sky over Tom's head.

"What will he do?" said Tom. "He can't come down here."

He looked up and saw the pilot's face through the big window. Then a door opened in the side of the helicopter, and a man came slowly down on the end of a line. Soon he was standing by Tom's side. He said nothing to Tom, and looked at Bill quickly but carefully. Then the man shouted in Tom's ear, "We can take *him*, but not *you*. He's ready now. I'll go up. When the line comes down again, fasten him on. We'll take him to hospital. You stay here. A party of climbers is coming up the other side for you. Do you understand?"

"Yes!" Tom shouted.

"Good! Don't forget. Fasten him on carefully. Like this."

Then the helicopter was pulling the man back. Tom waited. The line came down again. Tom took the end of the line and fastened it to the equipment Bill was now lying on. Tom stood back and shouted, "Right! Take him up!"

Bill went slowly up from the ground. The helicopter beat on in the sky over Tom's head. Bill was safe inside the door now. Tom stood on the mountain-side and watched. Then the tail of the helicopter turned round and it flew quickly away. Suddenly it was very quiet, and Tom was so tired he put on all the coats and slept, there in the snow, and he was still there when the party found him at ten o'clock that morning.

"Drink this," they said. "Eat this."

Tom drank the hot coffee and warmed his hands on the cup.

"Are you ready?" they said.

They took the camera which Bill used when he took the photographs of the two big birds. It was broken, but the film was still inside it. Tom took the cat fur with the bit of blood on it.

"Cats on the tops of mountains?" he asked himself.

They found the other camera and the binoculars in the snow on the other side of the mountain when they were going down.

Mary, Francis and Jane were standing near the telephone in the hotel when it rang again. Jane quickly picked it up and answered it. It was the doctor from the hospital.

"We have got your husband here. . . . He's broken his left leg. . . . He was very ill when they brought him in. . . . Yes, the bad weather and the cold on the top of the mountain for all those hours. . . . Is his friend there? The man who stayed with him? Not yet? When you see him, please tell him he did a good job. . . . Your husband? . . . Oh yes, he'll live. . . . Now, go to bed. Yes, that is the best thing. And sleep. Come and see him this evening. That will be the best time. He'll be more comfortable then. . . . But one thing is worrying me. He is talking about two big birds, two big brown and grey birds. . . . Perhaps you can help us. What is he talking about?"

Some people are always wrong

Tom knocked at the office door. From inside the office he could hear an angry voice. Then it was quiet, and then the voice shouted again. Mr West was speaking on the telephone. Finally the voice stopped. Tom knocked again.

"Come in!" shouted the man inside the office. Tom slowly opened the door. There, in the hot dirty room, was a big desk with three telephones on it. There was also a cup of cold coffee with a spoon in the cup, a piece of newspaper with a sandwich in it, and a basket full of pieces of paper.

"Don't stand there at the door!" shouted the man. "Come in!" Behind the desk sat a man with a big red angry face. He was wearing a dirty white shirt with no button at the collar, and a cheap yellow tie. His big hand, like a piece of meat, was still holding the telephone.

"Oh, it's you!" he said, in his angry voice.

"Yes, Mr West, you wanted me," said Tom. He was now standing in front of the big old desk, with its mess of coffee-cups, sandwiches, telephones and paper.

"Yes, I wanted you," shouted Mr West. "How long have you been working on this newspaper?"

"Three months, Mr West," said Tom.

"Three months," said his boss. "And tell me one job that you have done well in those three months!"

Tom said nothing.

"One job," said Mr West again. He held up one big finger and shook it in front of Tom's face.

"I don't know . . ." began Tom.

"You don't know!" shouted Mr West. "*I* know! There was that advertisement. I opened the newspaper, *my* newspaper, and read:

DON'T come to Walker's for good second-hand cars

and you put DON'T in big letters! Mr Walker took that advertisement out of the paper that same day."

"Well," said Tom, "I bought my car from him and I've had a lot of trouble with it. . . ."

"I know about your car. I'm telling you about that advertisement. Mr Walker paid us £20 a week for it, and now we've lost it."

Tom was trying to speak again.

"I've not finished," said Mr West. "Then I sent you to the police station when the police found the thief who stole the money from that train."

"I got the story," said Tom.

"Yes," Mr West stood up and hit the desk with his hand three times. "Oh, yes. You got the story. But you telephoned the wrong newspaper!"

"But I explained that, Mr West," said Tom. "The number of our newspaper office is 39632 and the number of the other office is 39532...."

"Don't say any more about it," said Mr West. "Then yesterday I sent you to the shop on Wood Road. An easy little job, wasn't it?"

"Yes, Mr West," said Tom.

"A job for a little child," went on Mr West. "The manager of the shop was giving a goldfish in a bowl to everybody who spent two pounds in his shop. That was all. A nice little story. Nothing difficult. And what did you do?"

"I can explain," began Tom.

Mr West did not listen to him. "What did you do? You drove your car through the front window of that shop!"

"But you told me that you wanted a quick story," said Tom. "I was trying..."

Mr West stopped him again.

"The story is on the front page of the other newspapers. Look!" And he threw down a newspaper on his desk in front of Tom.

"Look at that photograph!"

Tom looked. There was the back of his little car. There was the shop with its broken window. Tins of food were lying in the road. There was the crowd of people, and there was himself. A policeman was holding him up by one hand on the collar of his coat.

"It's a very good photograph," said Tom. "It was raining at the time, and quite dark and cloudy...."

Mr West could not speak, he was so angry. Like an actor in an old film, he slowly picked up the newspaper with the picture in it, threw it on the floor, and jumped on it.

Tom looked miserable. He could still see a piece of the picture, and the words:

Newspaper man drives through shop window

"Is my name in the paper?" he asked in a little voice.

Mr West sat down, picked up his sandwich, looked at it, and put it down again.

"Now, listen to me, Tom," he said finally. "I am going to send you out on a safe, easy, little job. There is nothing difficult or dangerous about this one. And, do you hear me, Tom? You must not make a mistake this time."

"Oh, no, Mr West," said Tom excitedly, "I'm sure I won't make a mistake."

"Now listen carefully," said Mr West. "Do you know the new Fire Station down at the end of Wood Road?"

"Oh, yes," said Tom. "I went past it yesterday when I was driving down to that shop. . . ."

"Don't talk to me about that shop," said Mr West. "I feel very ill when anybody talks to me about shops. Go to that Fire Station."

"Why?" asked Tom.

"Yesterday," said his boss slowly, "there was a big fire at the cinema. You must be the only person who has not heard about it. Go to the Fire Station and speak to some of the firemen who were there. Do you understand? Get a good story. When you come back, bring it to me. I'll be here."

Tom said nothing.

"What's wrong?" asked his boss. "You've got a pencil and your little notebook, haven't you?"

"Oh, yes," said Tom.

"Then go!" shouted Mr West. Tom went. He ran down to the front of the newspaper office and waited for a bus.

Half an hour later he was walking down Wood Road to the new

Fire Station. Outside, he saw the big red bell. Firemen in long boots were washing windows and doors. Others were cleaning and putting away equipment. Everybody was working hard.

Finally somebody said to him, "What do you want?"

"I'm from the newspaper," said Tom. "I've come about the fire at the cinema yesterday."

"Oh," said the big fireman in his coat and smart buttons. "Are you the man who drove his car through that shop window?"

"Yes," said Tom, "but I can explain . . ."

"Sandy!" shouted the big fireman to his friend. "This is the man who drove his car through that shop window yesterday."

The other man laughed. Big voices rang round Tom's ears. Six firemen stood round him.

"What's your name?" asked one of them.

"Where were you going when you drove into the shop?" asked another.

Tom told them.

"You wanted a story for your newspaper from the manager of the shop?" asked Sandy.

"And you drove your car through his window?"

"Yes," said Tom, "but . . ."

The six firemen laughed again.

"That's a good story!" they shouted.

"But wait," said Tom. "Please tell me about the fire at the cinema yesterday. I must have a good story for my boss, or I shall lose my job."

The six firemen were still standing round him. They came nearer.

"The bell rang," said Sandy.

"We put on our coats," said another fireman.

"And our boots."

"We drove to the cinema."

"We put out the fire."

"With water, Sandy."

"Yes, George, with water."

"Then we drove back."

"And here we are."

"Is that all?" asked Tom.

"No," said Sandy, "I lost a button from my coat."

"And are you very miserable about that button, Sandy?" asked George.

"I'm *so* unhappy about that button, George," said Sandy. "It was my best button."

Tom looked from one fireman to the other. They were all laughing at him. He had not got one word in his notebook. What could he do?

Suddenly the big red bell on the wall of the Fire Station rang! Tom put his hand over his ears. Firemen dropped brushes and equipment and ran here and there.

"Look out!" shouted a fireman, who was running past him.

"What's wrong?" asked Tom.

Another fireman ran by.

"Where's the fire?" shouted Tom.

"Here!" shouted the fireman.

"What?"

"Here, in the Fire Station!"

"A fire in a Fire Station," thought Tom excitedly. "Here's a good story!"

More firemen ran by.

"The fire's getting near the petrol," they were shouting. "Quick, Sandy! Turn on the water! We're ready now!"

Tom did not wait. He ran up Wood Road to the nearest telephone box. His hands shook as he put in the money.

"I must be right this time," he said to himself. "Three . . . nine . . . six . . . three . . . two. This is Tom," he said to the girl at the other end. "Mr West, please, quickly. This is something special." Then he heard the voice of Mr West.

"Is that you again, Tom? What do you want? Bring me the story. Don't telephone me."

"But, Mr West," said Tom, "this is a good story."

"Is it about the cinema?"

"No," said Tom, "this is a new story."

"Not the cinema?" asked his boss. "But I told you . . ."

"No, please listen, Mr West. This new Fire Station."

"Yes?"

"There is a fire there."

"A fire?"

"A fire in the new Wood Road Fire Station."

At the other end of the telephone line Mr West was quiet. He did not speak.

"Mr West!" shouted Tom. "Did you hear me?"

"It's not true," said the voice of Mr West in Tom's ear. He spoke slowly and sadly. "It's just not true. You've made a mistake." And he put his telephone down.

Tom threw his notebook on to the floor. Then he made the fingers of his right hand into a ball, looked at it, and then pushed it through one of the glass windows of the telephone box.